Solution Focused Practice in End-of-Life and Grief Counseling

Joel K. Simon, MSW, ACSW, BCD, has spent 30 years as a therapist and supervisor in varied settings. He has been a solution focused practitioner, trainer, and consultant for the past 17 years. Joel was trained in solution focus at the Brief Family Therapy Center in Milwaukee, Wisconsin, with the co-developers of the approach, Insoo Kim Berg and Steve de Shazer. He is a founding member of the Solution Focused Brief Therapy Association and has served as an annual conference chair and on the board of directors. Joel worked as the director of social work for Hospice of Orange and Sullivan Counties, Inc. Currently, he provides solution focused training, supervision, and consultation. Joel is the author of several articles on solution focus, including two with Insoo Kim Berg, and a frequent presenter at conferences. He is also the co-author of another book entitled *Solution-Focused Brief Practice with Long-Term Clients in Mental Health Services: "I Am More Than My Label."* Address comments and inquiries to joelsimon@0to10.net or visit www.0to10.net

Solution Focused Practice in End-of-Life and Grief Counseling

JOEL K. SIMON, MSW, ACSW, BCD

SPRINGER PUBLISHING COMPANY
NEW YORK

Copyright © 2010 Springer Publishing Company, LLC

All rights reserved.

No part of this publication may be reproduced, stored in a retrieval system, or transmitted in any form or by any means, electronic, mechanical, photocopying, recording, or otherwise, without the prior permission of Springer Publishing Company, LLC, or authorization through payment of the appropriate fees to the Copyright Clearance Center, Inc., 222 Rosewood Drive, Danvers, MA 01923, 978-750-8400, fax 978-646-8600, info@copyright.com or on the Web at www.copyright.com.

Springer Publishing Company, LLC
11 West 42nd Street
New York, NY 10036
www.springerpub.com

Acquisitions Editor: Jennifer Perillo
Project Manager: Newgen
Cover design: Mimi Flow
Composition: Newgen

Ebook ISBN: 978-0-8261-0580-6

09 10 11 12/ 5 4 3 2 1

The author and the publisher of this Work have made every effort to use sources believed to be reliable to provide information that is accurate and compatible with the standards generally accepted at the time of publication. The author and publisher shall not be liable for any special, consequential, or exemplary damages resulting, in whole or in part, from the readers' use of, or reliance on, the information contained in this book. The publisher has no responsibility for the persistence or accuracy of URLs for external or third-party Internet Web sites referred to in this publication and does not guarantee that any content on such Web sites is, or will remain, accurate or appropriate.

Library of Congress Cataloging-in-Publication Data

Simon, Joel K.
  Solution focused practice in end-of-life and grief counseling / Joel K. Simon.
    p. ; cm.
  Includes bibliographical references and index.
  ISBN 978-0-8261-0579-0
  1. Terminally ill—Mental health. 2. Solution-focused brief therapy. 3. Grief therapy. I. Title.
  [DNLM: 1. Counseling—methods. 2. Bereavement. 3. Professional-Patient Relations. 4. Terminally Ill—psychology. WM 55 S595s 2009]
  RC451.4.T47S56 2009
  362.17'5—dc22
                                                                    2009033509

Printed in the United States of America by Hamilton Printing

*To my wife, Joanna; son, Michael; and daughter, Alicia:
you have given meaning to this adventure we call "life."*

*To the blessed memory of my mother, Fanny Simon:
she gave to me the tools that help me take on life's challenges
with a sense of humor, energy, and determination to forge ahead.*

*To the memory of Steve de Shazer and Insoo Kim Berg:
mentors, role models and colleagues.*

Contents

Foreword ix
Preface xi
Acknowledgments xv

PART I: INTRODUCTION   1

1   Hospice: History and Philosophy   3
Historical Antecedents   3
Hospice History in the 20th Century   5
　　Case Study One: The Local Community Perspective   8
　　Case Study Two: The State and National Perspective   13

2   The Historical Context of Solution Focused Practice   23
Steve de Shazer   24
Insoo Kim Berg   27
Brief Family Therapy Center   27
Solution Focus and Orange County, New York   29
The Future of Solution Focus   32

PART II: PRINCIPLES AND PRACTICE OF SOLUTION FOCUS   35

3   Use of Language in Solution Focus   37
Theory   38
Meaning Making   41
Language-Games   46
The Role of Emotions in Counseling   48

4	**Principles of Solution Building** 51	
	Problem Solving vs. Solution Building 51	
	Problem Solving 52	
	Solution Building 55	
	Solution Focus Stance 58	
	Solution Focused Assumptions 59	
	Brief vs. Short-Term Counseling 68	
	Co-Constructing Goals With Clients 70	
	Customership: The Counseling Relationship 73	
5	**The Tools of Solution Building** 75	
	Solution-Building Questions 76	
	Troubleshooting: Common Issues in Solution Focused Practice 95	
	Evaluating Outcomes: The Post-Discharge Survey 97	
	Proviso 104	

PART III: APPLYING SOLUTION FOCUSED BRIEF PRACTICE TO END-OF-LIFE AND GRIEF COUNSELING 105

6	**Stories of Healing: Solution Focus and the Dying Patient** 107	
	Life Review 107	
	Denial 108	
	Conclusion 125	
7	**Expect the Unexpected: Solution Focus With a Widowed Client** 129	
	First Session 130	
	Second Session 136	
8	**The Other Woman: Solution Focus With a Bereaved Family** 141	
9	**Changing Perspectives: Solution Focus With a Bereaved Client** 157	
	Session One 157	
	Session Two: E.A.R.S. 170	

Afterword: Eulogy 179
References 183
Index 187

Foreword

When I was in my first job as a young doctor, an old colleague taught me two phrases that he said had been his guidelines for a lifetime of work. The first phrase was: "Most diseases heal despite the treatment" and the second one was: "The primary purpose of the health care industry is to produce a need for health care." Since I have spent most of my professional life in the mental health business, I have changed the latter into "The primary purpose of the mental health industry is to produce a need for mental health care."

In 1969, Elizabeth Kübler-Ross wrote about death and described five stages in the process of dying (denial, anger, bargaining, depression, and acceptance). These stages then eventually became stages of grief and since then many psychologists, psychiatrists, and psychotherapists have used them as a frame for listening to clients. "In what stage is he?" "Is he progressing normally?" "Is he stuck in a stage? If so, which one?" The stages quickly became yet another very useful tool for pathologizing the different ways people react and respond in situations of grief and loss, thus producing a need for mental health care.

I share Friedman and James's[1] experience:

> Many grievers tell us that a mental or medical health professional "strongly suggested" they were in the *denial* stage, when all they'd said was that they were having some difficulty since Mom died. Even after reiterating they were clear that Mom had died, the therapist insisted they were in denial.

At first glance, this is a book about the hospice movement and about how solution focused work can be applied in that context. But it is much more than that. It's a book about hope and growth in the face of death and loss. It is a book about possibilities – not finalities. Perhaps most

---
[1] Russell Friedman, John W. James. The myth of the stages of dying, death and grief. *Skeptic*, 2008: Volume 14:37–41.

important, it is a book about all the different ways that people deal with loss and bereavement – no way being the right or the wrong way – and how solution focused brief therapy can be helpful in making sense of the experience that people go through when facing death or accompanying a family member or friend who is facing death.

So here is the power of solution focused practice. Solution focused practitioners ask their clients: "How do you want to act, feel, think, and interact?" "What of this are you already doing?" "What is useful for you to do, think, and feel at this point?" They trust their clients' answers and build dialogues with their clients around these questions. They know that clients have their own unique way of doing what they need to do and knowing when they are doing what is right for them. Solution focused practice de-pathologizes the person who, because he or she is treated as capable and competent, therefore becomes just that. Joel Simon's book is evidence of this.

Harry Korman, MD

Preface

> True hope is swift, and flies with swallow's wings;
> Kings it makes gods, and meaner creatures kings.
> —*William Shakespeare,*
> **Richard III,** *Act V, Scene 2*

No matter where I worked, my assumption has always been (at least for the past 16 years) that solution focus will be applicable, and that it is my job to apply it to the context. Hospice of Orange and Sullivan Counties in Newburgh, New York employed me in May, 2005. I immediately set out to discover the applicability of solution focus in this new context.

The application to bereavement counseling seemed to be a natural for me, but I have to admit I was not sure of how it was going to be applied to individuals facing end-of-life circumstances and their significant others. Having the opportunity to discover the applicability of solution focus to this population was an exciting prospect for me. Once again, I approached it with the assumption that it would work, and I was to discover how.

The staff had been briefed prior to my arrival that I was interested in and practiced solution focus. It was not my intention to immediately advocate for a solution focused approach; I had learned very early that solution focus was a very different paradigm from those in which most professionals had been trained. My own experience, and the experiences of others who have been more or less successful in developing a solution focused approach in various systems, suggested that it was best to go slowly. This was reflected in a chapter I wrote with Thorana Nelson (2007) entitled "Meta-Systemic Considerations of the Solution focused Brief Approach":

> The essence of the SFBP approach is a deep respect for the resources, abilities, and worldview of those with whom we work. This not only includes

our clients, but also extends to our colleagues and the intra- and intersystems with which we communicate. It does little good to insist on shining the "light of truth" on those who hold a different view. (p. 153)

When I first met with the social work staff as their new supervisor, they expressed a curiosity about solution focus. In fact, one of the social workers had recalled that I had presented a solution focused lecture to a psychology club at a local university. As an undergraduate student, she had been in the club at the time. I agreed to provide a series of presentations on solution focus to the hospice social workers. This included not only didactic material, but actual video case examples as well.

As would be expected, not everyone was interested in solution focus as his or her modality. Several of the social workers, however, began to incorporate solution focused interventions into their practices. There were a few who were interested about the prospects and began to use solution focus in their practice with individuals facing end-of-life situations.

There was one particular social worker who was very skeptical in the beginning. Some time later, she was faced with a family where the husband/father was terminal, and this served only to exacerbate an already conflicted family system (see Chapter 6). The man asked the therapist to meet with the family to deal with issues of "communication" within the family.

The social worker approached me asking what she should do. I suggested that she meet with the family and simply follow a solution focused format: how they will know that the sessions were being helpful, what differences they would notice, how would those differences make a difference, the Miracle Question, scaling, taking a break, and returning with compliments and a between session suggestion.

The social worker returned after the family meeting and announced that the session had exceeded her expectations. She went on to marvel at how the family was able to go beyond the conflict and begin to entertain the idea that, even in the face of a limited time frame for the husband/father, change was possible. The social worker's story is not unique. Other staff that had entertained the idea of using solution focus principles were reporting similar results.

When I initially entered the hospice system, the social workers were unclear about their roles. During the first staff meeting, I had asked them what is it that they do that is different from the volunteers who also meet with patients and their families. There was much hesitation in answering that question, and I realized that my direction was clear – to help them rediscover what made them unique as social workers. I believe, to a large extent, that solution focus provided them with tools and principles that were congruent with traditional social work values.

I wrote this book because I believe that solution focus provides an approach and valuable tools to naturally help those who face life-limiting conditions co-construct possibilities rather than limitations, and provides hope and comfort in a time of despair. When I broached the subject of the book to Yvonne Dolan – an author, presenter, and solution focused practitioner in her own right – her immediate response was that this is a book that needs to be published.

Chapter 1 explores the history and philosophy of the hospice movement beginning with Ancient Greece, moving through the Middle Ages, the Renaissance, the twentieth century first in the United Kingdom, and finally the United States. It includes an interview with a CEO of a local hospice, his involvement and thoughts about the current state of the movement including the issues that now face hospices on the local level (and, no doubt, will continue to face them in perpetuity). The chapter also includes an interview with a woman who was involved both on the state and national levels in the early introduction of solution focus to the United States.

Chapter 2 details the history of solution focused brief practice (SFBP), its influences, and its prime movers: Steve de Shazer and Insoo Kim Berg. It traces the history from Dr. Milton Erickson and the Mental Research Institute in Palo Alto, California in the 1950s to the pioneering work of de Shazer beginning in the early 1070s, and his eventual collaboration with Berg that culminated in the establishment of the Brief Family Therapy Center (BFTC) in Milwaukee, Wisconsin. The chapter takes us up to the present day and the establishment of the Solution Focused Brief Therapy Association (www.sfbta.org), and its role in furthering the work of BFTC both before and after de Shazer and Berg's death.

Chapter 3 lays the foundation of solution focus philosophy through post-structural thought. Chapters 4 and 5 describe the basic concepts and tools of solution building. Chapter 6 is about the application of solution focus to clients with life-limiting conditions and their families. Chapters 7 through 9 put it all together with three case examples including actual verbatim taken directly from video recordings. The first case example is of a man with a very surprising story and outcome. The second is of a family that came for one session only. The final case is of a woman whose mother died a year prior, and who saw me for two sessions.

The ultimate goal of the book is to challenge the reader's assumptions about work with clients with life-limiting diseases and their families, and bereavement work. Further, the book serves to show that solution focused brief practice can be a useful approach in end-of-life and bereavement work.

J.K.S.

Acknowledgments

My thanks to Yvonne Dolan and Terry Trepper who encouraged me to write this book. To the staff of Hospice of Orange and Sullivan Counties who teach about life and hope. To the clients and families of Hospice who paid me the honor of letting me into their lives and allowing me to learn from them. To my friends and colleagues of the Solution Focused Brief Therapy Association who constantly provide me with a source of support, knowledge, and inspiration.

Special thanks to Gale Miller for reviewing and making suggestions on Chapter 4. Also special appreciation to my daughter, Alicia (the artiste and art teacher), who provided the illustrations in Chapter 4.

Introduction

PART I

1 Hospice: History and Philosophy

There is a tide in the affairs of men
Which taken at the flood, leads on to fortune;
Omitted, all the voyage of their life
Is bound in shallows and in miseries.
—*William Shakespeare,*
Julius Caesar, Act IV, Scene 3

HISTORICAL ANTECEDENTS

According to Kohut and Kohut (1984), the word "hospice" is derived from the Latin *hospitalis* translated to "of a guest." According to Siebold (1992), there are earlier antecedents to the modern day hospice movement that date back to 1134 B.C. and ancient Greece. Temples were created for weary travelers and "custom dictated that they be clothed, fed, and entertained with no questions asked" (p. 13). There is evidence that a special facility specific to the dying was in operation in India around 225 B.C.

The Christian era brought with it an emphasis on the care of the sick and dying: "Christian tradition, particularly Catholicism, held preparation for death and the afterlife in high regard" (Siebold, p. 14). The 100 years of The Crusades served to spread the concept of hospice throughout the known world. By the thirteenth century, the number of hospices numbered about 750 in England, 40 in Paris, and 30 in Florence (McNulty & Holderby, 1983). At that time, hospices were established as facilities for weary travelers and crusaders.

The Renaissance brought with it an emphasis on the scientific method as it especially applied to medical treatment and cure. It is not surprising that as a result, "Research-minded physicians working in hospitals believed that their function was to cure diseases, not to provide supportive services for the dying poor or respite for the weary travelers" (Siebold, p. 20). During this period, there were few new hospices and many of the established hospices were converted to hospitals where the focus was on research, treatment, and cure. The dying and poor were relegated to almshouses and workhouses created for that purpose – no doubt, more a matter of out-of sight and out-of-mind rather than treatment and cure. This is reminiscent of Scrooge's statement in *A Christmas Carol*. When asked for a donation for the poor, he responded:

> Are there no prisons? And the Union workhouses, are they still in operation? I help to support the establishments that I have mentioned – they cost enough, and those who are badly off must go there.

When the reply is, "Many can't go there, and many would die." Scrooge responded, "If they would rather die, they had better do it, and reduce the surplus population." The irony here is that the poor and dying were given care during the Middle Ages. Given that medical treatment did not exist, death was commonplace and, therefore, accepted as the natural course of life.

With the advent and growth of medical science, death became the taboo subject that it is today. This is not to suggest that we would have been better off if the Renaissance never happened and if society had remained stagnant in the Middle Ages. Had medical science never evolved, life would have been short marked by the struggle for survival and governed by plague, disease, and superstition. Certainly, advances in treatment and care have resulted in greater longevity and a higher quality of life. However, with the prospect of treatment and cure, the subject of death is to be avoided even though the treatment of terminal conditions results in an improved quality of life.

The interest in hospice was renewed in the 18th century for two probable reasons: 1) the Irish potato famine and 2) the recognition by the clergy that those with terminal illnesses were being warehoused in institutions with less-than-humane conditions (Siebold, op. cit.). Our

Lady's Hospice, which opened its doors in Dublin in 1879, was the first facility to provide palliative care for the dying. The establishment of the hospice was a result of the work of Sister Mary Aikenhead of the Irish Sisters of Charity.

HOSPICE HISTORY IN THE 20TH CENTURY

The Hospice Movement in the United Kingdom

According to Kohut and Kohut (op. cit.), Sister Mary Aikenhead also was the prime mover for the establishment of St. Joseph's Hospice in 1905 in London: "She considered death to be the beginning of the final pilgrimage. She called her nursing home after the medieval respite – *hospice*" (p. 6).

The hospice concept took hold in the United Kingdom throughout the first half of the 20th century, sparked especially by Dame Cicely Saunders. Dame Saunders was originally trained as a nurse but a back injury prevented her from further pursuing that career. She returned to school and retrained as a social worker.

In 1946, Dame Saunders was working at St. Thomas' Hospital when she came in contact with David Toma, a Polish Jew. In an interview with *The New York Times* (Stolberg, 1999), she reflected back on this meeting:

> I met a Polish Jew from Warsaw, who got out before the Resistance. He was 40, and had inoperable cancer, and because he had no family, I knew he had run into trouble. And so I kept in touch with him, and when he collapsed and was admitted to another hospital, I followed him there and was virtually his only visitor for the 2 months that he was dying. We talked together about somewhere that would be more suitable for him than the very busy surgical ward where he was. We wanted a place not just for better symptom control, but for trying to find out, in a way, who he was. (p. 1)

Toma bequeathed Saunders 50 pounds toward establishing a facility dedicated to end-of-life care. It was this experience that motivated Saunders to enter medical school to train as a physician. Upon graduation, she was hired as a medical officer with St. Joseph's Hospice.

In 1963, with a grant from St. Thomas' Hospice in London, Saunders visited 18 facilities in the United States. As part of this lecture series, Saunders showed slides of patients before and after hospice treatment. The "before" slides showed the patients physically affected by their respective illnesses. The "after" slides depicted patients who were clearly able to maximize whatever time was left for them (Siebold, op. cit.).

Saunders' lectures had a profound effect on those who came to hear her speak and, if not the main impetus, certainly her lectures were a major reason for the growth of the hospice movement in the United States.

The Hospice Movement in the United States

Separate from Saunders' work was that of a psychiatrist, Elisabeth Kübler-Ross, who was truly a pioneer in the study of death and dying. With much resistance from the medical establishment, which viewed her interest as ghoulish, Kübler-Ross would interview those with terminal diagnoses to learn of their experiences, thoughts, and feelings. The culmination of those studies was her first book, published in 1969, *On Death and Dying: What the Dying Have to Teach Doctors, Nurses, Clergy and Their Own Families*.

In 1966, both Kübler-Ross and Saunders were invited to lecture at Yale University Hospital by Florence Wald, Dean of the Yale School of Nursing. Saunders addressed the spiritual and physical aspects of care; Kübler-Ross presented the results of her end-of-life conversations (Siebold, op. cit.). According to Siebold, "Had Kübler-Ross not become involved in the movement, it might not have become as popular as it did.... Kübler-Ross made the public sit up and take notice of death and dying" (p. 73).

Based on the work of the Yale Study Group, the Connecticut Hospice in Branford, the first established hospice in the United States, began serving the terminally ill in their homes in 1974. The Connecticut Hospice was funded through a grant from the National Cancer Institute with the goal of creating a national demonstration center for home care of the terminally ill and their families.

William Lamers, a psychiatrist, who had a personal experience with grief, sought to use his training to help others through their bereavement. According to Siebold (op. cit.), Lamers met Kübler-Ross and based upon her suggestion, founded the Hospice of Marin in California, the first Medicare-certified hospice in the United States.

In 1972, Kübler-Ross testified before the U.S. Senate Special Committee on Aging. She spoke of the isolation of those with terminal illnesses and, in general, the manner in which society denies death. Two years later, Senators Church and Moss introduced legislation to provide funding for hospice programs; unfortunately the legislation was not enacted.

In 1978, a U.S. Department of Health, Education, and Welfare task force reported:

> The hospice movement as a concept for the care of the terminally ill and their families is a viable concept and one which holds out a means of providing more humane care for Americans dying of terminal illness while possibly reducing costs. As such, it is the proper subject of federal support. (2003, www.nahc.org, p. 2)

The Centers for Medicare and Medicaid Services (CMS) initiated a demonstration project in 1979 of 26 hospices across the country to assess the cost effectiveness of hospice care. The secondary goal was to determine specifically what services hospices should provide to patients and their families. In 1980, through a grant from the W.K. Kellogg Foundation, the Joint Commission on Accreditation of Hospitals (later changed to Joint Commission on Accreditation of Health Care Organizations – JACHO) set out to develop standards for hospice accreditation.

Congress finally approved a provision to create a Medicare hospice benefit in the Tax Equity and Fiscal Responsibility Act of 1982. Because of its concern for cost containment, the Act included a cap on both annual per-patient expenses and inpatient hospitalizations. The CMS established a daily reimbursement rate under the hospice benefit program.

In 1989, the Government Accounting Office (GAO) released a study showing that only 35 percent of eligible hospices were Medicare certified. They listed several reasons why hospices chose not to seek certification, including the major reason: the low reimbursement rates. At this time, there were an estimated 701 Medicare-certified hospices that provided end-of-life services to approximately 61,000 patients with an average stay of 44 days (Hospice Association of America, 2003, p. 2).

By 1993, there were 1,288 certified hospice programs. The major increase in certified programs was in home care, agency-based, and freestanding hospices. At this time, the average cost per patient was "still significantly less than the Medicare hospice cap" (ibid., p. 3). In 2000, the Office of the Assistant Secretary for Planning and Evaluation of the U.S. Department of Health and Human Services and the Urban Institute released a study entitled, "Medicare's Hospice Benefit: Use and Expenditures." The study confirmed that hospices provided cost-effective end-of-life care.

Case Study One: The Local Community Perspective

Dan Grady has been the CEO of the Hospice of Orange and Sullivan Counties since 1988. While he has been CEO, he was involved in the planning stages prior to the hospice's certification. Mr. Grady's story is an example of the process that many hospices went through just after the demonstration period and prior to certification. The interview with Mr. Grady took place on June 4 and June 18, 2008. Mr. Grady received his Bachelors of Social Work and Masters of Business Administration from Iona College.

Joel: *When did you first hear of hospice?*
Dan: It was during my orientation to the Hudson Valley Health Systems Agency (HVHSA), a health care planning agency I was working with. HVHSA was set up by the federal government across the country to add local input to health planning. They started in '76 and ended about 1985 but the state continued it on for another 5 or 6 years. It was where you came if you wanted to add anything in the health care arena: drug beds, hospitals, nursing homes, and home care. We were responsible for the seven counties north of New York City. We were the first level of approval. It was a state/federal match. Essentially it was a quasi-governmental agency. We reviewed and approved all new health entities in Orange County. Hospice was one of the new ones, so I had in-services on hospices with the rest of the team. Soon after I started there in the mid-80s. I think we started doing reviews in '85. In '84 we had just heard about them.

In '85, because of the CON (Certificate of Need), we really had to start researching them – getting the mission, scope, the cost, and the 3-year projections. It's a competitive mix; you have to do a little more work because you want to make sure that what everyone is telling you is true. It was very competitive. For example, in one county's case, there were two consultants who were instrumental in the establishment of the National Hospice Medicare Benefit, Don Gates and Lou Westbrook, who became the founders of the hospice known today as Vitas – which is the largest in the United States. On the other side was a consultant from New York who was one of the first and founding members of the state association. An HVHSA board member (a volunteer), our director, and I had to hold numerous discussions with both parties on a potential merger of the project – some of these meetings became very confrontational. Therefore, as the lead staff person, I had to learn all about both projects to function effectively in this environment. There was a lot of homework involved; the board packets were literally 3 inches thick.

Joel: *How long did you work there?*

Dan: I started in '84 and left in '88 to work here.

Joel: *So, basically, your contact with hospice was what you were doing at CON.*

Dan: HVHSA was the first organization to recommend approval; from us, it went to the state health department.

Joel: *How did you go from there to CEO of hospice?*

Dan: It was about '86. I worked on hospices and then I worked on home care. I could see that the health systems agencies' days were numbered. I started looking around. This hospice had gone through enough and they were ready to hire somebody. Being someone with some experience (at least I knew how to say the word), going through the hurdles of starting hospices, and someone who had the connections, they decided to give me a shot.

Joel: *At the point you came in, what was hospice like?*

Dan: At the beginning of this company?

Joel: *Yes.*

Dan: There was a pre-existing group which voted itself out of existence. So in January of 1988 through February there was a new incorporation of a new nonprofit. At that point in February, I was hired as the first CEO and staff person. The other four people worked separately although we combined as a group. Technically there were two CEOs for a period of time. So our job was to get the policies, procedures, and manual. So by July we could have a pre-opening survey. Then we had to hire a staff. At that point, we were 100 percent grant funded. We went fee-for-service in July 1988. That was a big transition. A good number of our existing volunteers refused to continue and get the required health screenings. When we went under the Department of Health, they needed physicals and they couldn't quite understand how they were seeing Mrs. Smith for 2 years; now they needed a shot.

Joel: *At the point, you came into hospice, what was the staffing like?*

Dan: There were five: The social worker was doing volunteer coordination (that's all they really had), bereavement, and counseling. He ran volunteer support groups around the county, he ran the volunteer training. The spiritual care person did a lot of public speaking about hospice, and seeing patients. There was a nurse who did assessments but we weren't doing medical care. Finally a bookkeeper and a clerk. The whole budget was about 100 thousand [dollars]. The first year we doubled the budget. We went to the county and got some grants. The county helped out; United Way helped out.

Joel: *How many patients did you serve that first year?*

Dan: Oh, we were so proud! We started with five. We went to 10; 5 of those 10 were on hospice for 6 months. At the end of the year, from July to December, we served 39 people. One day last year we had 139 people on the program. There were three part-time nurses including a part-time nursing director. In 2 years, we were up to 40 or 50. We thought that's where it would end. We had four people showing up for our first team meetings even though we gave no services. We met for 3 hours.

Joel: *Doing what?*

Dan: I don't know, but we knew everything about everybody.

Joel: *So when you started there was no direct patient care.*

Dan: That's what we added when we went from Department of Education to the Department of Health. This took a couple of years because it required developing a Certificate of Need (CON). Up to that point, they were doing nothing else but volunteer and bereavement. We couldn't do the hands-on nursing care until we were certified. We would go in with public health nursing. They would do the medical end.

Joel: *When did hospice finally become certified?*

Dan: July 1988. By the time I was hired, we already had the CON. It took 2 years to finally get a pre-opening survey. That was done by the state on behalf of the federal government.

Joel: *When you came did you have a particular orientation or model?*

Dan: We already knew about the concept of an interdisciplinary team. That had already been established. We used the concept of interdisciplinary team and everything else was built around that.

Joel: *Personally, where did you want to take hospice?*

Dan: My orientation was business. We had to think of it as a business. I had to make sure we had the supports: for example, bookkeeping, office. Within 2 years, we had computer support, new accountants; we did a lot more work with fund raising and we developed corporate plans.

Joel: *When you first came here, hospice basically served Orange County, is that right?*

Dan: No, we were Orange County before we started. When we started, we found because of the merger of the two CON into one, the two from Florida I talked about before had plans for one hospice for Dutchess, Orange, Ulster, and Sullivan Counties. Once a neighboring hospice started, we pulled back.

Joel: *How did we end up becoming Orange and Sullivan Counties?*

Dan: There was a separate hospice in Sullivan County that was started about a year after ours. It never achieved a sustainable census. Within a year, they were in major trouble financially and in terms of quality, in trouble with the Health Department – they were there 1 minute and gone the next. We were asked to go in and do something but I knew that there could be potential legal issues so we couldn't merge our corporations; our board would not have approved it. At that point, we were not able financially – we were living from Medicare check to Medicare check. It worked out 2 years later.

Joel: *What are the challenges that face this hospice?*

Dan: We've done great in donations this year, but operationally – survival mode. That's the biggest short-term thing; we have to get out of our own way. For example, when we decided to build a residence, I explained to the Board that we're going to lose money, it's a new business, you know [it'll take] 3 to 5 years. But Boards and executives find it very hard to actually live through the projected lean years. Now they realize, "It's really big money!"

Joel: *Businesses go through periods of consolidation and expansion. I assume we're in that consolidation phase.*

Dan: I've never had to consolidate before. As bad as things were those 10 years, we staffed up appropriately because we were up. Other hospices have increased their staff when they were up only to lose staff when they were down. How long will we continue to be successful [retaining staff]? I don't know.[1]

Joel: *What do you see for the future? In general, where do you see hospice as a movement going?*

Dan: If we don't do more in this nation about the quality of hospice, we're in trouble. Don Shoemaker (the president and CEO of the National Hospice and Palliative Care Organization) says you have a movement, you have a dream, you have an industry and then you have a gimmick. What does that mean? When we were losing money, we didn't have any charlatans getting into the business. All of a sudden we did a good job of lobbying and we got to the point where some hospices were making money. At a state conference, a mother and

---

[1] In fact, my position was eliminated several months after this interview.

her son were overheard stating, "Mother and I are in concrete. But now we know that hospice is to go where you want to make money, so, we're getting our own hospice."

Joel: *So that's another challenge…*

Dan: Quality.

Joel: *We're diluting the movement.*

Dan: Some hospices give good service and some do not, but there are both for-profit and not-for-profit hospices in both camps. How can you have a state like Mississippi have an average stay of 111 when everyone else is at 50? How can states like Mississippi and Oklahoma have more hospices than the state of New York? You make the system work – that's the gimmick part. I'm one of the few nonprofits that will say that there are some good for-profits. The challenges are money, governmental oversight. We have good quality indicators. In some rural areas of the country where the money is drying up, the quality indicators are going down. So where does that leave us? Well, whom can I merge with? The answer is probably to merge with someone stronger than you are, not as weak as you are. If we had one hospital system in the county, I'd probably be part of it. I would have had us put in years ago. But we have three systems and seven hospitals.

Joel: *How much has managed care affected us?*

Dan: Not at all. They love us. Why? Because we keep people out of hospitals – 160 dollars a day reimbursement versus a thousand [dollars]. And we do a better job of that than most hospices in this state very few hospital days.

Joel: *Five or ten years from now, where would you want to see the movement?*

Dan: We're at a danger point now – it all depends where we cross the tracks. I actually think we would be better off if we had more oversight. I just wish that those that oversee us would remember that if you regulate an industry, you have to protect it because you take it out of the free market. There's a difference between a planner and a regulator. Previously, the people who came from the state were trying to make you better. Now they're just trying to make sure that the paper trail looks good. Where would I like us to be in 5 years? Well first, out of debt [laughs].

Joel: *What about the movement in general – across the country?*

Dan: I'd like to see less hospices with higher quality. I care less about ownership than about quality of service.

Joel: *What about in terms of public acceptance?*

Dan: I would like less fear. Hospice is the dead word. I'd like people to say, "Go there, you'll have a great time!" "They came, they laughed with us, they paid for things, they made our lives easier." We're here to make their lives easier; we're here to make you [sighs]. I would love it that people wouldn't have less choice as it is now – "Come on hospice or give up other stuff." Is that going to happen? No, but as long as you asked what I would like, that's it. I would like to be able to say, "Well, we have a palliative care program that's well funded." We could get them on palliative care and then convert them to hospice. I would like for the government to be more consistent. You have to have equal enforcement of the law.

Joel: *Why isn't it consistent on the federal level?*

Dan: Because the federal government subcontracts oversight with each state. Some states you only get surveyed upon opening and never again. Some hospices only do the minimal required by the states. Some states, for example, don't mandate social work visits.

Joel: *Is it possible to provide a quality program and still make enough money to break even?*

Dan: Probably not in this county – we're too close to New York City.[2] Maybe I should be more worried about money, but it's the quality that bothers me. If quality indicators go down, we'd have to do something. The fact is if you give better care, more people will come to you. By the same token, one hospice giving poor care may taint the rest of us.

Case Study Two: The State and National Perspective

Carol Selinske had been an active community organizer working on the local, state, and national levels to help promote hospice, secure funding, and negotiate hospice regulatory policy. Ms. Selinske had worked with the New York State Hospice Association for 17 years. The interview took place on June 30, 2008.

Joel: *What is your current position?*
Carol: I'm retired since 1998.
Joel: *Prior to your retirement, what were you doing?*

---

[2] Orange County, New York, is about 65 miles north of New York City. While the Medicare reimbursement rate for New York City hospices is higher than Orange County, the cost to Hospice of Orange and Sullivan Counties for providing services is equal.

Carol: Working backwards: I was the interim director of Hospice of Westchester. Preceding that, I was doing special projects for them.

Joel: *Your own educational background?*

Carol: I have a Bachelor's from SUNY in human services administration and women's literature. I went back to school in my mid-40s because I hadn't finished. At that point, I was Executive Director of the New York State Hospice Association and needed to put some sort of degree in my resume. So I went back and finished.

Joel: *Prior to your involvement with hospice, what were you doing?*

Carol: A lot of volunteer community work. In 1977, I had gone to a national church conference and someone there was talking about community projects that worked. One group was talking about starting a hospice. That was the first time I had heard about hospice. When she described what that was, it was like the proverbial light bulb going off. I just had an aunt who died very, very badly. So I came home looking for people to start a hospice with – or help start a hospice. There were a few volunteers who were trying to get something going in New York State, but the state was resisting having hospices or any other new programs. I began by taking notes for the committee and one thing just led to another.

Joel: *What was this resistance based upon?*

Carol: Well, it's a complicated case in New York because it's one of the most heavily regulated states. The Health Department had just come off a huge nursing home scandal just prior to that in which they had failed to adequately monitor what nursing homes were doing. So they had no interest whatsoever in a whole new field to monitor and survey and they pointed out, somewhat fairly, that each time the legislature gave them new duties, it did not give them more money to do them with. They just viewed this as another way to look bad if a scandal occurred. In their view, terminally ill people were already getting adequate care. So the Health Department played games with the legislature off and on from the late seventies until '84. In 1984, we got the federal bill passed as part of the National Hospice Association's legislative taskforce. Once that was passed, then the state would be turning down federal money if they did not allow hospice.

Joel: *So, basically, you started by getting a group of volunteers together.*

Carol: In the late 1970s, there was already a small committee of doctors and nurses in Westchester County, New York. Unbeknownst to us, in upstate New York, there was a group in Buffalo around the same time and a small group just outside of Albany. At that point, I started calling around the state to find out if anybody else was doing this. That became the coalition that became the New York State Hospice Association (NYSHA) and later the Hospice and Palliative Care Association of New York State (HPCANYS). I think we held our first meeting around 1979.

Joel: *How many people showed up for that meeting?*

Carol: Surprisingly, a lot. I would say at least 50 or 60, maybe more. People began to come out of the woodwork. We had just not been aware of each other's efforts initially.

Joel: *The U.S. taskforce came out about 1978, I believe.*

Carol: That's right.

Joel: *They started the demo project in '79.*

Carol: That's right. Things had already started under the table, but, yes.

Joel: *You mean there were already funded programs?*

Carol: No, not funded.

Joel: *When you say "under the table," what do you mean?*

Carol: Groups had already started that were affiliated with nursing agencies; reaching out and sort of doing hospice. They were getting geared up so when it became legal they would be ready. Meanwhile, [they were] caring for patients in a hospice-like way.

Joel: *I interviewed Dan Grady, the CEO of Hospice of Orange and Sullivan Counties; he recalled that it was basically a volunteer program in the early '80s and the medical care was being done by outside nursing agencies.*

Carol: Right. I recall up in Buffalo, it was led by Charlotte Shedd. She was at the heart of just going ahead and doing it. Other nurses were afraid to do that for fear of losing their licenses. But Charlotte said, "Fine, let them come and shut us down and take my license and we'll see how much the newspapers like the idea of dying people being refused free care because the Department of Health (DOH) doesn't want them to have it." Of course the DOH backed off because that certainly would have been bad press. In some ways, it took skill, but it also took nerve. She was a very conservative person whose husband [was] a surgeon who went right ahead and did this with her. I believe the DOH initially gave Hospice Buffalo a home care license to get around the problem.

Joel: *What was the original staffing like?*

Carol: Well, I didn't work for a hospice at that point. I worked for what was essentially a lobbying and educational group, even though we didn't call ourselves that. The group split. There were those who didn't want to go ahead with organizing [a] political movement but just wanted to do patient care. There were those of us who thought the only way to change things was to go to Albany [the capital of New York State] and keep working the political end and the national end as well, since at the time the chair of the Senate Finance Committee in Washington was a New York senator, Daniel Patrick Monahan. So, New York pressure was key to moving things in Washington. As I said, once that happened, New York State couldn't sit on it any longer. We played political games, getting it through one House but not the other until that happened. At that point, I was working for Hospice of Westchester, a largely educational group. We were going around, beating the drum for hospice, doing presentations, preparing printed materials, going to Albany and kept knocking on doors. We found some good supporters in Albany on both sides of the aisle. But that was [a] many-years-long process. We put together annual educational and caregiver conferences. I was also engaged in getting the program started from the Visiting Nurses end in White Plains. Ultimately the state and national organizing effort became too large and we needed a New York State Hospice Association. I took that on. We did all the educational and lobbying things. At that point, in every county in New York, there was somebody who wanted to start a program – somebody out of a nursing agency, hospital, or a community group. NYSHA took on fund raising and strong technical assistance so we could provide people with experts to consult where needed. The group became NYSHA formally in 1984, I think.

Joel: *So, it sounds like this was pretty much on-the-job training.*

Carol: Learning as I went, yes. I would go to D.C. and sit in with Health Care Financing Agency (HCFA), look at the draft regulations, and talk to people about what we thought we were going to do. Then I would come back to New York State, do workshops, and be introduced as an expert. In reality, I was only 2 weeks ahead. It was just a matter of being dogged.

Joel: *Where was New York State in terms of the demonstration period?*

Carol: Behind. I'm not sure when it started in New York. I do remember that, at first, most demonstrations were hospitals. The excuse was that hospitals could gear-up faster. That actually wasn't true as it happened. In reality, the DOH felt that they could monitor hospitals more easily and DOH was nervous about what they didn't know.

However, the first Medicare-certified hospice in New York State was Hospice of Schenectady, a community-based program.

Joel: *The group you were working with, when did they become part of the demonstration?*

Carol: I am not sure of the date. At that point, I had left the local group. Like a lot of institution-based programs, the local hospital-based program mistakenly thought a lot of money would come with this. When they found out there wasn't going to be any money, they sat on their approvals until they knew where the funds were coming from. That was certainly understandable but at the same time demoralizing.

Joel: *How did this get promoted to the public?*

Carol: Well, we did everything we could to get in newspapers and to get on television and radio. At one point, I managed to interest Frank Fields, who was then on the *CBS Morning Show*. Donald Gaetz came as a representative of the national movement and did a rousing presentation. We were even able to get it into *The New York Times* sporadically.

Joel: *What was the public's response?*

Carol: There was an immediate resistance from some groups that assumed that this was somehow related to euthanasia. For the most conservative Catholic and Jewish groups, the idea of giving up "life saving" care for comfort care was an anathema. We worked hard to keep ourselves out of the euthanasia debate – and the patient's right to self-determination debate – which we had to enter in the end. I remember one fellow when we were doing Living Wills and Health Care Proxies in Albany. The phrase from his report was "this Pac Man of self-determination gobbling all before it." I'll never forget that phrase. We had been trying to work with him until I saw his report. I didn't quite realize that what he really objected to was people having a right to determine their fate. That was our original problem – separating ourselves from euthanasia.

Joel: *Yes, I suppose that was the big challenge along with the political and financial.*

Carol: Yes, and they're all intertwined.

Joel: *Were there any other challenges that you recall?*

Carol: Those were the three big ones. In way, we were probably one of the best, if not the best, organized state in the country simply because the DOH was so *opposed to it*. In a way, it served us very well. Because they were so totally unreasonable, people had to band together even if they didn't agree on everything, and work with a united front. So it was a double-edged sword. In response, we were organizing, adding new members, and getting great support. It was harder to come by in other states where health departments were not as aligned against them. That wasn't the DOH's intention, but that's how it worked.

Joel: *When it first started, what was the original model like?*

Carol: The original goal of the people I worked with and a lot from around the state was that this would come out of independent, free-standing, home care type organizations. It quickly became mixed. People who worked in hospitals would have a very difficult time trying to turn around not only the financial questions, but ingrained physician practices where physicians ruled the roost. Some people from home care agencies thought that this would just be an extension of what they did for which they could do fund raising. They could get a feather in their cap and not change their services much. When the federal regulations came out it became clear that all programs would have to provide full hospice services or stop using the word "hospice." The big challenges for community groups were not having an organizational base and money.

Joel: *How much were you involved on the national level?*

Carol: A lot. My good relationship with Daniel Patrick Monahan's [senator from New York] staff and ultimately a good relationship with the New York-area Health Care Finance staff helped a lot. The founding mothers, Florence Wald in Connecticut and Dr. Jo Magno on the national level, were extremely well-educated and motivated health care professionals who really saw this from a spiritual end as well. They all knew Cicely Saunders. We invited Saunders here to inspire others. But many of the founding mothers didn't understand and didn't want to understand the political process. This was somehow dirty, tainted, and not pure hospice. What they would have liked to have done was to have (as was explained to me) a 10-year prolonged demonstration with a few hundred or thousand patients here and there to show its worth. When everyone would come to understand its worth, there would be funding. But the train was leaving the station – both New York State and the federal government were writing the regulations. This was going to happen and they could either get on the train or be left far behind. There wasn't going to be any 10-year demonstration. Unless these founders took a part in this process, it was going to resemble something they didn't like at all. At that point, there was a division. Some very savvy business, political types on the national scene, Don Gates and Hugh Westbrook, popped up. When the national group formed, it named Dr. Magno as its first CEO. Gates and others were actually able to get considerable funding to get this going on the national level. Dr. Magno went about doing inspirational speeches but not doing the work necessary to form a strong organization. So there was a prolonged period of infighting and disorganization. The National Hospice Organization,[3] which was what it was called then, went through three or four CEOs and was deep in red ink. Each time they hired a CEO who did well what the last one didn't, but this one didn't do what the last one did well so one big piece of it would fall through the cracks. They finally got Jay Mahoney who was a financial person from a hospice in Colorado. He came in, took control, and got the organization back on financial footing. The business-type people – Don Gates and, to some degree, Hugh Westbrook – gained influence [and] got the organization into an effective lobbying and organizing group. So, some of the founding mothers at that point wandered away with hurt feelings. I sound unsympathetic, but I'm not. They put their hearts and souls into this and were the initial spark. But when one of these women tried to talk me out of lobbying, she sounded as if I had chosen to sell my body on the street. Her whole tone was, "How could you do this? You're a nice person." So, that was a big division. From my perspective, while it was very painful and some of the founding mothers dropped out, it had to happen.

Joel: *I guess it never would have gone as far as it did without the political activism.*

Carol: Right. How are you going to get Medicare funding? How are you going to get decent regulations so that you can have a balance between providing good care and being so heavily regulated that you can't do good care?

Joel: *Was part of the issue that the U.K. model was very different from the U.S. model?*

Carol: Yes, the U.K. model was paid for – that was the big difference. In the United Kingdom, inpatient care didn't have to be as strictly limited. It could be a place and not a program or it could be a place with a program. In this country, regulators wanted it to be a program that could use a place. It was a very different model. Cicely Saunders, much like Mother Theresa, is taken by followers to be this very

---

[3] Now called the National Hospice and Palliative Care Organization (NHPCO).

spiritual person – which she was. What they chose not to view was what a really canny political person she was. She worked her model and fed it into the British health care system. It took her decades to get where she was. Some people here just wanted to see just the feel good stories – the spiritual model – and not do all the grinding work that Saunders did.

Joel: *What was the difference between your initial vision of hospice and what happened to that once you started realizing the reality?*

Carol: I don't know that I had a vision other than people not dying in needless pain and isolation. I thought the doctors, nurses, and social workers would figure that out. The more I sat with them and went to workshops with them I realized that they were on the right track. What we would have all liked to have seen was hospice centers with home-like settings that could take 8 or 12 patients and less restriction on inpatient care to augment a strong home care component. That would have been the ideal – and it still is in some ways. But most hospices have found absolutely no way to finance this. I have forgotten the exact figures but when we figured the initial Medicare rates, the assumption was about a 60-day stay. The rate worked out at that because all the intensive expense in the first 1 or 2 weeks was then mellowed out in a relatively calm period before the intense expense of the last weeks. The average stay at that point turned out to be something like 27 days and the median was worse – something like 19 or 21 days. So, the whole model was off. From the beginning, the federal government said "You all have come forth as volunteers, you sold this to us as having a very strong community volunteer aspect to it. Well, then, you have to prove that this is true. This can't be just another fund-raising, expensive, hospital program." That's what the regulations limiting inpatient care and for the volunteer component were all about. Existing programs couldn't just tack on one volunteer and say, "Look. We have volunteers, we are a hospice." The federal government also assumed that you were going to do community fundraising – it was going to be cost effective for them. That's the whole balance. Of course, the overhead in the hospital, especially if the step down is not in your favor, can be egregious. But they have the population base. Home care overhead is probably more reasonable but you don't have the population base. You don't have the hospital to draw on unless they're really referring to you appropriately. Many were not, especially if they had their own home care programs to refer patients to.

Joel: *From your perspective, what are the current challenges facing the hospice movement?*

Carol: I haven't been following it closely but I think that it is the same tug and pull. It's not the spiritual-minded founding mothers anymore. It is more of a business-like approach. But I don't think that's an altogether bad thing – you're more likely to stay afloat. Zelda Foster was the first president of NYSHA. Two years ago, HPCANYS was having an anniversary and she was invited to go, as was I. My impression was there was more of a division between the program leaders (the CEOs, the financial people) and the nurses, social workers, etc. The ideal in the beginning was this very close knit team all pulling in the same direction. While professionalizing the organizations was necessary, it sadly went back to a more traditional health care model in many cases, especially as the larger programs grew. The administration and the line people became very separate. Maybe that was inevitable, but it's too bad.

2 The Historical Context of Solution Focused Practice

> When beggars die, there are no comets seen;
> The heavens themselves blaze forth the death of princes.
> —*William Shakespeare,*
> Julius Caesar, *Act II, Scene 2*

Miller and de Shazer (1998) state that it might be useful to think about solution focus as a rumor: "a series of stories that circulate within and through therapist communities" (p. 364). The authors remind us of the children's game called "telephone" (or "gossip") where one person whispers a secret to another and so on down the line of several people. When the secret finally reaches the last person in line, it holds little similarity to the original. Likewise, the telling of the solution focus story is passed down from person to person, most often in training sessions such as those I have conducted.

Miller and de Shazer warn that the article is not meant to be the one true version of solution focus but "a contribution to the evolution of the solution focused rumor" (ibid.). Likewise, this chapter is not meant to be the definitive history of solution focus. It is composed of what others have written, and conversations and training with de Shazer and Berg, of which I am fortunate to have been a part. This chapter continues the tradition of adding to the rumors of solution focus.

STEVE DE SHAZER

The logical place to start is with Steve de Shazer. de Shazer originally graduated with a degree in music from University of Wisconsin in Milwaukee; he studied jazz saxophone. However, he was a voracious reader and especially enjoyed philosophical concepts. One of the books he read was *Strategies of Psychotherapy* by Jay Haley (1963). Cade (2007) quotes de Shazer:

> Until I read this book, as far as I can remember, I had never even heard the term, "psychotherapy." Certainly, this was the first book on the topic that I read. I enjoyed it perhaps more than any other "professional book" I'd read in philosophy, art history, architecture, or sociology.... It is not going too far to say that these two books [the other was *Advanced Techniques of Hypnosis and Therapy* by Jay Haley (1967)] changed my life and shaped my future. (p. 43)

de Shazer returned to the University of Wisconsin and earned his Masters of Science in Social Work (MSSW) in 1971.

The aforementioned books interested de Shazer in the work of the innovative psychiatrist, Milton Erickson. The thread of Erickson's ideas weaves throughout the basic principles and practices of solution focus. de Shazer (1985) states, "In short, brief therapy can be seen as the refinement and development of Erickson's principles for solving clinical problems" (p. 13).

Observation and Utilization

When I first arrived at a new job as a treatment coordinator in an inpatient psychiatric center, I spent the first two weeks in the adult unit in order to learn the system. A couple of days after I began, I noticed that I was scheduled to lead a group that the director of the unit had entitled "solution focused group." The group was sandwiched between two problem-solving groups. I made a comment on the anomaly of having a solution focused group just after and before problem solving groups. This somehow led to a discussion on the place of theories in psychotherapy practice. The unit director insisted that you had to have a theory as a starting place for practice.

Erickson's approach suggested that significant and lasting change happens when therapists observe and utilize the client's own resources.

Further, it is not necessary to understand the root causes of the client's problems for such change to take place (ibid.).

Contrary to the unit director's theory about theories, Erickson began with the client, not a theory, as the focus of therapy. de Shazer and a sociologist, Joseph Berger, spent many hours reviewing tapes of Erickson, trying to find an underlying theory. de Shazer (1999) recalls that there were too many exceptions and that, indeed, Erickson did not have a Theory.

Cooperation

de Shazer (op. cit.) quotes Erickson regarding cooperation:

> As Erickson put it in 1965: to elicit the cooperation of the patient one ought to be permissive for best results. One really ought to ask the patient to cooperate in achieving a common goal. You should keep in mind that that common goal is a goal for the welfare of the patient wherein the patient is cooperating with you to achieve something that primarily is of benefit to him. (p. 80)

The research and work of the Mental Research Institute (MRI) in Palo Alto, California, also had a profound influence on de Shazer (Cade, 2007). MRI was established in 1958 as a research organization born of a grant obtained by the anthropologist and major proponent of cybernetics, Gregory Bateson. Other members included John Weakland, Jay Haley, William Fry, Paul Watzlawick, Richard Fisch, and Don Jackson.

In 1966, the Brief Therapy Center was created within MRI as a center for family therapy. They described their approach as focused problem resolution (de Shazer, 1991). At a time when the structural therapies field burgeoned, the Brief Therapy Center stood out as a group moving in a very different direction. Until then, the general approach to family therapy utilized the basic medical model approach that was inherent in psychodynamic psychothcrapy; mainly the perceived need to understand what motivated the family members to act as they do, and then to change the family structure. In contrast, brief therapy approaches as exemplified by MRI's work, focused on what therapists learned solely by observing the family's behavioral interactions and then intervening accordingly.

It must be remembered that the major influence on MRI, and later the Brief Therapy Center, was not psychological but anthropological. Psychology attempts to explain behavior; anthropology observes and describes behavior. This is congruent with Erickson's admonishment to observe and utilize. It is also no coincidence that MRI was very much influenced by Erickson, as well, especially Erickson's use of pattern disruption. In regard to this, Simon and Berg (2004) state:

> One of Erickson's primary approaches entailed first learning the problem pattern and then prescribing a small change in the pattern. Several of the researchers at MRI, among them John Weakland, Jay Haley, and Gregory Bateson, were interested in Erickson's work and especially in his use of pattern disruption (de Shazer, 1991). These researchers saw problems as socially contextual and reasoned that an individual's social situation serves to maintain a problem. Accordingly, they strategized ways of disrupting a problem pattern. (pp. 133–134)

de Shazer's conceptual approach to therapy was influenced by the work of Ludwig Wittgenstein and the co-constructionists (see Chapter 3).

In 1972, de Shazer was living and practicing in Palo Alto. It was during this year that he first came in contact with John Weakland from MRI, who had a profound effect on de Shazer's conceptual model (Simon & Berg, 2004). At the time, de Shazer was working with clients using a one-way mirror and collaborating with a sociologist, Joseph Berger, from Stamford University.

In 1976, John Weakland invited de Shazer to participate in a conference entitled "Techniques of Brief Therapy." de Shazer reflected on this the first time he presented his ideas to an international audience (Simon & Berg, op. cit.):

> The audience thought it rather peculiar, or unorthodox, that we would ask the client about what the problem was and further that we would take their answers seriously! This sort of dissonance between what I think of as normal and ordinary and what the audience thinks unorthodox and/or bizarre has continued but the dissonance lessened over the years as I have become used to it. (p. 134)

de Shazer described (Berg & Simon, ibid.) how, in 1977, a therapist was working in front of the one-way mirror. The team called in with a suggestion and the therapist disagreed. The therapist explained to the patient that he needed to excuse himself and consult with the team. The therapist returned to reflect to the patient the team's thinking and this seemed so helpful to the client; the standard practice of taking a session break was born.

INSOO KIM BERG

The other major co-developer of solution focus was a first generation Korean, Insoo Kim Berg. Insoo was trained in Korea as a pharmacist and came to the United States to further her training. She was introduced to social work, a profession that was absent in her country of origin. Much to her parents' dismay, Insoo pursued a career in social work and graduated in 1969 with her MSSW from the University of Wisconsin at Milwaukee.

In 1974, Insoo was working in a family therapy clinic in Milwaukee. She was interested in MRI's work and traveled to Palo Alto to train with John Weakland. While there, she had a couple of extra days and, rather than sightseeing, she asked Weakland if there were any other clinics at which she could observe therapy behind a one-way mirror. John, of course, mentioned the work Steve was doing and that led to the first meeting between Insoo and Steve. They were to become both life and business partners.

BRIEF FAMILY THERAPY CENTER

Steve returned to Milwaukee in 1978 and was working in the same clinic as Insoo. They began using a one-way mirror to research therapy until several of the other staff began to complain that what they were doing was unethical, claiming it violated the client's confidentiality. While the use of video cameras and mirrors are much more commonplace today, this certainly was not true at that time. The director asked them to cease and desist, so Insoo and Steve began to do their therapy in the evenings instead. After the director again complained, Steve resigned and began to see clients in his and Insoo's home.

A therapist would interview the client in the living room. Another member of the team would stand on the stairs leading to the second level with a video camera. In turn, the camera was cabled to a reel-to-reel video recorder attached to a monitor in a bedroom. The rest of the team watched the session, the therapist would take a break, consult with the team, and return to relate the team's thoughts and ideas to the client.

Insoo and Steve took out a second mortgage on their house and with the funds had enough money to rent and equip an office and hire support staff for six months. During the final plenary of the 2003 Conference on Solution Focused Brief Practices, Insoo recalled that time, stating that it was "make it or break it" and described how she had many sleepless nights during the beginnings of the Brief Family Therapy Center (BFTC).

The original "core team" at BFTC consisted of De Shazer, Berg, Eve Lipchik, Elam Nunnally, and Alex Molnar. Marilyn Bonjean, Wallace Gingerich, John Walter, and Michele Weiner Davis later joined the group (de Shazer, 1985).

Several research projects were completed during this time, each seminal in the development of the approach. Steve and sociologist Elam Nunnally studied the effect of session length on outcome. They restricted the session to 30 minutes, including taking the break. de Shazer (1999) recalls this collaboration:

> In none of the 40 or so cases did we have trouble designing an intervention message. We always found that we had "enough" information. Furthermore, this arbitrary time limit had no effect on outcomes, task performance, or on whether or not the client would return for the subsequent session. (p. 12)

The research served to refocus the work from time to content.

In another project, they viewed tapes and live sessions, first asking the question, "What is it that the therapist does that is helpful to the client?" and later refined to, "What are the therapist and client doing together that is helpful to the client?"

de Shazer and Berg's original intent during the early days of BFTC was to establish an MRI of the Midwest. However, the research at BFTC began to move them in a different direction – at least with a different emphasis. As de Shazer (1988), Berg, and their colleagues continued to observe and work with clients, they came to realize that many clients reported exceptions (times that the problem is either absent or less bothersome) to the issues that impelled them to seek out help. Some clients reported that the exceptions happened spontaneously, while others stated that the exceptions were as a result of deliberate action. This observation was to have two major effects: 1) it moved BFTC away from MRI's focused problem resolution approach, and 2) it negated the assumption that the problems clients report are constant.

The team's discovery and focus on exceptions furthered the development of "focused solution development" and diverted them from the MRI model. de Shazer (1991) writes:

> The focused problem resolution model focuses on interaction sequences in the present. It is aimed at describing attempted solutions that failed, i.e.,

efforts that are accidentally maintaining the problem, and it attempts to intervene to stop those efforts. The focused solution development model, which is related and yet distinct from the focused problem resolution model, also focuses on interactional sequences in the present and is aimed at describing exceptions to the rule of the complaint and prototypes or precursors of the solution that the client has overlooked, thus intervening to help the client do more of what has already worked. (p. 58)

In 1982, Wallace Gingerich suggested that they call what was developing at BFTC "solution focused therapy." De Shazer insisted that the title be expanded to "solution focused brief therapy" (see Chapter 4).

de Shazer wrote his first book, *Patterns of Brief Family Therapy*, in 1982. The book interested a number of practitioners in what was developing at BFTC and many came to Milwaukee to sit behind the mirror and watch SFBT taking place. In the later part of the 1980s and through the mid-1990s, there was an expansion of interest in and of activity at BFTC. Steve and Insoo, joined by other members of the training faculty, provided periodic training sessions. They and others continued to research and write articles and books about the practice, which in turn interested more therapists in the approach.

In the early 1990s, BFTC was a fully operating clinic and training center. The patients treated there were similar to those that were referred for therapy in community mental health clinics. As the interest in solution focus grew, so did the demands on Berg and de Shazer's time. There were many requests for training and consultations not only in the United States, but also in Europe and Asia.

In 1998, Steve came to visit the clinic in which I was working along with my colleagues, Dan Gallagher and Janet Campbell. After the visit, as I was driving Steve to a conference in Manhattan where he was presenting, I asked him to estimate how much time he spent outside of Milwaukee doing training and consultations. He replied that, cumulatively, he was away from home about 10 months of the year. Because of the growing demand on his and Insoo's time, the decision was made to close BFTC in the autumn of 1994.

SOLUTION FOCUS AND ORANGE COUNTY, NEW YORK

My first contact with solution focus came in March, 1992. At that time, I was in the middle of an advanced training in Ericksonian psychotherapy and hypnosis. The county where I was living and working had several outpatient clinics. Most of the therapists were using time unlimited theories and the caseloads were capped. If a potential client contacted the intake person, he or she would have to wait about three months for an intake appointment, and another three months for a first appointment with a therapist. Concerned about the growing waiting list, the county began looking for short-term approaches that they hoped their clinicians would be interested in adopting.

A director of one of their clinics was married to a woman in a psychology doctoral program. She had returned from training at BFTC and brought back a tape of Insoo working with a client. The clinic director and his supervisor listened to the tape and, based upon what they heard, sought out a solution focused trainer. A five-day training session was scheduled and all county clinicians were required to attend. Among them were a few clinicians from other agencies who were also invited to attend; I was one of those.

My immediate thought was that I was already involved in the Ericksonian training and I did not relish being out of my office for five days. I intended to attend the training for a polite one or two days and then excuse myself. The first day peaked my interest. After the second day, I knew I needed to know more, and by the third day, I was beginning to incorporate solution focus into my practice.

When I returned to the clinic, I taught what I had learned to the therapists with whom I was working. They were also interested and we began to experiment with the approach. We would place a video camera in an office, run a cable to an adjacent office, and connect it to a VCR and monitor. In this way, we were able see some of the therapy clients using a team.

About four or five months after my initial training, I learned of a solution focused trainer and practitioner, Dan Gallagher, who was living in a neighboring county. I contacted him, and we eventually hired him as a consultant, meeting with staff once a month. Dan's own enthusiasm for solution focus and what we were developing even motivated him to come on his own time and work with us behind the mirror.

In 1994, upon Dan's urging, the then BFTC administrator visited the agency and was impressed as well. There was some conversation and even a written proposal for a connection between the BFTC and the agency with which I was involved. The administrator invited me to a four-day advanced training at BFTC. Unfortunately, as mentioned previously, BFTC closed its doors a year later.

Chapter 2 The Historical Context of Solution Focused Practice 31

My wife, son, daughter, and I packed ourselves into the family's Honda Civic and drove out to Milwaukee from New York State in July of 1994. I was part of a group of 25 trainees, most from foreign countries including Korea, Canada, and Switzerland. This was the first of three training programs with Insoo and Steve that I was fortunate to have attended, but the only one at a functioning BFTC – the center closed that fall.

The county eventually privatized one of their clinics and the agency I was working for at the time was chosen to take over its operation, and I was asked to direct that clinic. I learned several years later that one of the major reasons the county awarded the license to my agency was because of my interest and commitment to solution focus, and the agency's guarantee that I would be its director. Several of the staff that we hired were already interested in solution focus. Since the clinic was already equipped with a one-way mirror, we began to see some clients as a team.

When we moved to a new space, it was equipped with a large team-training room, an interview room divided with a large one-way mirror, and audio/video equipment. I began to offer training sessions to clinicians within the agency. Eventually, I received calls from outside clinicians requesting training as well. The agency established the Center for Solution Focused Brief Therapy Training, and we held several well-attended training sessions throughout the year. We were also contacted by other solution focused practitioners who planning to be in the area and wanted to be part of our team. As previously mentioned, Steve de Shazer visited the clinic in 1998, as well as Harry Korman from Sweden and Insoo Kim Berg. During her visit, Insoo commented that our clinic and training center was reminiscent of BFTC in the early 1990s.

In the fall of 2001, Steve de Shazer and Terry Trepper, chair of the graduate program in family therapy at Purdue University in Calumet, invited 30 solution focused trainers and practitioners to Purdue University to share training ideas – I was, again, fortunate to be included among them. We came together as a group several times in 2001 and 2002. During one of our meetings in the autumn of 2002, it was suggested that we form an association with the sole purpose of planning an annual conference on solution focused practices: the Solution Focused Brief Therapy Association (SFBTA) was soon incorporated as a not-for-profit entity.

The first SFBTA conference was held in November, 2003, in Loma Linda, California. Information about SFBTA, previous and future conferences can be found at the association's website, www.sfbta.org.

Steve fell ill on route to Vienna and died on September 11, 2005 with Insoo by his side; Insoo passed away January 10, 2007. The decision about who was to continue their work fell to Insoo's daughter and sister, who had been an original member of the BFTC board of directors. It was their decision to choose SFBTA as the steward for Insoo and Steve's legacy. The SFBTA board of directors posts the following on the SFBTA website:

> The SFBTA gratefully and humbly accepts this gift and the confidence invested in us. The exact shape of our inheritance will evolve over the next months and years. We will continue to pursue our original mission of fostering growth of solution focused practices. Our conferences, remaining a central focus, are dedicated to the fundamental principles of equality, collaboration and interaction among participants. In addition, having been given the rights to the BFTC teaching video and audio tapes, we will insure that they remain available in contemporary format to those who wish to learn the model. The association is committed to supporting those who wish to cultivate new applications and take their mastery of SFBT to the highest level. To that end, in the spirit of the original founders meetings, we will continue to develop learning opportunities of quality.

THE FUTURE OF SOLUTION FOCUS

The interest in solution focus continues to grow. More and more programs in social work, family therapy, counseling, and psychology have begun to include solution focus as part of their curricula. While the mental health system in the main still remains wedded to the medical model, there have been some inroads for the inclusion of solution focused ideas. SFBTA is a vibrant organization and the annual Conference on Solution Focused Practices is well attended. Each year's program reflects the growing diversity of solution focused practices. It is my opinion that solution focus has not yet hit its stride.

While SFBTA has become central to the legacy of solution focus, there is no longer a training center where people can come and watch solution focus in operation. This may need to be the next step in the development of the approach. The public, in general, has been so saturated with the medical model that solution focused ideas are counterintuitive to them. It may be useful to strategize ways of educating the public about solution focus.

If successful, there will be an increased demand for the approach, and this, in turn, might motivate clinicians to learn more about solution focused practice. Of course, this is always a double-edged sword. As an approach becomes more popular, there are those who are unscrupulous enough to label themselves solution focused while actually practicing from a more traditionally problem-solving stance. While the general attitude has been to avoid certifications (and I personally agree with this), there will need to be a way of protecting the public so that if they choose to work solution focused, they can be sure that the clinician practices solution focus.

Principles and Practice of Solution Focus

PART II

3 Use of Language in Solution Focus

> There are more things in heaven and earth, Horatio,
> Than are dreamt of in your philosophy.
> —*William Shakespeare,*
> **Hamlet,** *Act I, Scene 5*

Language is, by its very nature, vague and imprecise. Clients come to us complaining of "having depression" or "poor self-esteem" and wanting to "get through the grieving process," "move on," or "go back to being my old self." "Depression," "self-esteem," "the grieving process," "moving on," and "old self" have no meaning until the client and the clinician co-construct[1] the meanings together through language.

de Shazer (1991) states, "perhaps the best that therapists can do is creatively misunderstand what clients say" (p. 69). It is this creative misunderstanding that holds out the possibility that the conversations that clinicians and clients have together might prove in some way useful to the clients – and perhaps the clinicians, as well.

Likewise "theory," "post-structuralism," "meaning," and "language-games" are imprecise terms, for they are bound by the limits of language. As Wittgenstein (1922) states it: "The limits of my language are the limits

---

[1] I am using the term "co-construct" to mean a process of mutual meaning making that occurs between the clinician and the client. The significance here is that the clinician's expertise is in developing a conversation that is useful for the client. The clinician is not an expert on meanings.

of my mind" (p. 21). This chapter represents my misunderstandings of Theory,[2] post-structuralism, meaning, and language-games. Thus far, these misunderstandings have been useful to me; hopefully, the reader will strive for useful misunderstandings as well.

THEORY

Insoo Kim Berg was working with a woman expressing hopelessness regarding her situation. Berg strove to find the smallest hint of positive possibilities to exploit to no avail. Finally, the woman exclaimed that in order for things to get better, a miracle would have to happen. Berg suggested that the woman consider that possibility and the rest of the session was focused on what would be different because of the miracle and how it would make a difference to the woman. The team observing the session was excited about the question and they decided to ask each client about his or her personal miracle vision. Thus, the Miracle Question was born (Cade, 2007; de Shazer et al., 2007; Simon & Berg, 2004).

From the onset, solution focus was an inductive approach where the interventive tools were created by listening to the client, and learning what the client and clinician do together that would make a difference for the client. Solution focused practice was developed (and continues to be developed) *in vivo*. This is a radical departure from how more-traditional approaches were developed.

Traditionally, clinicians are taught the language of a Theory, or a series of related Theories, and the client is understood within the context of that Theory. It is thought that the advantage of a Theory is that it provides some guidance to the practitioner and may serve to inform the clinician's interventions. I believe that this, in fact, may provide a false sense of security and may serve to complicate and obfuscate the work.

Insoo Kim Berg (personal communication, 1997) once said that the questions we ask our clients not only get information but give information, as well. What we ask clients tells them what we are interested in and directs their attention. There is a tendency to view that which does not fit within the context of our Theories as mere static to be ignored. As such, we risk ignoring useful information that may suggest possible solutions.

---

[2] In this chapter, I am using Theory with a capital "T" to connote a meta-theory; that is, a theoretical approach that requires a specialized language and a set of practice rules that must be learned if one is to subscribe to that particular Theory.

If, for example, we follow a Theory that dictates that the key to problem solving is gathering problem information – further, the probability of discovering *the* solution to the problem is directly proportionate to the amount of information about the problem – then we are likely to regard as unimportant any information from the client about exceptions to the problem. The Theory dictates what we will or will not pay attention to and directs the client to do the same.

Because the client is now socialized into our particular theoretical stance, he or she will most likely view the world colored by the clinician's Theory. If the approach is one that is oriented to "understanding" the problem, the client will spend the time in his/her everyday life looking for the problem to report experiences back to the clinician at the next visit. Because of this focus, events in the client's life that previously would not be construed as having any relationship whatsoever to the problem may now be viewed by the client as part of the problem system.

de Shazer and colleagues (2007) reflect this tendency for Theories to control direction:

> In other words, if a patient's dream is analyzed, then at the end of the interpretation the therapist and patient will discover that the dream was a wish fulfillment. The next patient reports a dream and the therapist does an analysis but this develops into an interpretation that is not wish fulfillment. Does this mean that the theory is wrong and not all dreams are wish fulfillments? No, this means that, in some way or another, the analysis was wrong, because the therapist holds the belief that all dreams are wish fulfillments and, and therefore, a mistake must have been made in analysis. (p. 103)

We have come to understand that it is not necessary to have a Theory in order to practice good therapy (Simon & Nelson, 2007). While others may disagree, the simple fact remains that good clinicians practice good therapy independent of the presence or absence of a theoretical orientation. Similarly, a complex and all-inclusive Theory does not in and of itself create good clinicians.

We could construct a view of the world as being "both/and." For example, my personal experiences and my experiences with those I have counseled tell me that the processes of grieving and healing occur simultaneously, yet we are trained to view our experiences through the lens of "either/or." If we are trained to see only the bereavement, we are sure to miss the healing. The question then becomes, does "complicated bereavement" exist as a real phenomenon or is it more the product of training? To quote Wittgenstein (1958), "With different training the same ostensive teaching of these words would have effected a quite different understanding" (p. 5).

The other problem with subscribing to a Theory is the danger of becoming cognitively inflexible. Theories often engender fierce loyalties and their adherents are highly competitive, claiming that their Theory is the one true path. Two anecdotes may serve to make this point.

In my early career, I attended a seminar entitled "Introduction to Psychoanalysis." The seminar leader, a graduate of a prestigious psychoanalytic institute, arrived one day very excited and reported how in the monthly meeting of their psychoanalytic society, one of their inner circle suggested a small variation on the definition of the concept of defense mechanism. The result was a general uproar within the society's membership with one faction siding with the leader and the other practically accusing him of heresy.

The other story involves a clinical agency that was established under Jewish auspices. The agency was directed by a major funding source to hire an expert in Jewish law and practice. The CEO of the agency at that time was highly resistant to the idea and stated, "Freud is my religion."

Within the circle of solution focused practitioners we have often had debates about whether solution focus represents a Theory for practice. I am fully on the side of the argument that does not view solution focus as a Theory.

The dictionary (Abate, 1997) defines theory as "supposition or system of ideas explaining something, especially one based on general principles" (p. 831). I may (and, in fact, I do) have some theories (with a small "t") about why solution focus works, but these are mine alone. Other practitioners may have similar or different theories (or none at all, preferring to remain descriptive). However, there is no meta-explanation of why solution focus works.

There may be some attempt to suggest that poststructuralism (explored later in this chapter) is the Theory of solution focus, but one need not learn or subscribe to poststructural philosophy to practice solution focus. Finally, poststructuralism is not explanatory, but rather descriptive, of what happens when clients and clinicians hold conversations together.

Wittgenstein (1958) states:

> There must not be anything hypothetical in our considerations. We must do away with all *explanations* and descriptions alone must take its place.... These are, of course, not empirical problems; they are solved,

rather, by looking into the workings of our language and that in such a way as to make us recognize these workings: *in despite of* an urge to misunderstand them. The problems are solved, not by giving new information, but by arranging what we have always known. (p. 47)

My experience suggests strongly that solution focus works best when it is practiced both simply and descriptively.

MEANING MAKING

We can define how language functions from two polar opposite points of view[3]: structural and poststructural. Each will determine how we view the client, view our role, and define the purposes of the conversation. Further, each will determine what happens next for both parties, since action follows from orientation.

Structuralism and Meaning[4]

Elizabeth's mother died a year ago from ovarian cancer. Elizabeth was very close to her mother and while Elizabeth expected the death, she was surprised by her reaction. She had withdrawn from social contacts, and when not at work (where she reported being frequently distracted), spent her time sitting alone at home thinking about her mother, going through old family photographs, and "compulsively" replaying videos. Upon the urging of her friends, her employer, and other family, she made an appointment to see a bereavement counselor.

Elizabeth explained to the bereavement counselor what she was experiencing and doing. Elizabeth told the counselor that she just wanted to be happy again, but the sorrow and grief were just overwhelming. She needed to "work through" them in order to get on with her life. The counselor, trained and interested in an object relations theory, postulated that Elizabeth's grief was being complicated by a clinical "depression" as a result of an early childhood failure to completely separate/individuate from her mother. The mother's death was the precipitant for raising anew Elizabeth's failure to completely differentiate.

---

[3] There are several ways to define language; for the purposes of this book, I am exploring two.
[4] It should be noted that I am using the terms structural and poststructural in the context of clinical work only. Different fields of study make different meanings of these terms.

Essentially, according to the counselor, this was a differentiation problem. The counselor's theoretical stance prescribed that the focus of the work would be to help Elizabeth explore the history of the relationship with her mother and, through this and the resolution of the inevitable transferential relationship, come to gain insight into the etiology of her complicated grief and her need for greater separation/individuation, and strengthened boundaries.

A structural orientation is encapsulated within this hypothetical case. The counselor's theoretical view is that Elizabeth's complaints are symptoms of a deeper problem – a deficiency in the early childhood process of separation/individuation. This stance prescribes that the counselor must help Elizabeth gain insight into her interpsychic processes.

de Shazer (1991) states:

> Structuralist thought points to the idea that symptoms are the result of some underlying problem, a psychic or structural problem such as incongruent hierarchies, covert parental conflicts, low self-esteem, deviant communication, repressed feelings, "dirty games," etc. (p. 31)

Simon and Nelson (2007) address the structural orientation to treatment:

> From a structuralist perspective, our jobs as therapists are, in part, to assess and discover "truth" by asking questions and eliciting descriptions of symptoms of underlying problems.... Asking about childhood experiences, for example, is more likely to elicit evidence of lack of differentiation than would questions about current effects of the client's complaint. (p. 158)

In the structuralist's cognitive world, the meanings of words are fixed. We can use terms such as depression or complicated bereavement and assume that the other person understands what we mean because the meanings of such words are independent of their conversational contexts.

In *Republic*, Plato (Jones, 1969), an early Greek structuralist, postulates that there are two realms: the world of sense and the world of forms, which have neither space, physical reality, nor time.

Marias (1967) gives an example of the Platonic world of forms using a sheet of paper that is almost white:

> When we say that something is *almost white*, we deny it absolute whiteness by comparing it to something that is unconditionally white; that is, in order to see a thing is not truly white, I must know already what whiteness is. But

since no visible thing – neither snow, nor clouds, nor foam – is absolutely white, I am referring to a reality that is distinct from all concrete things, the reality of total whiteness. (p. 44)

For Plato, following a long tradition of philosophical structuralism, there is the world we can sense and a greater reality of ideal forms. Of course, 2000 years later, René Descartes' famous quote is probably the finest example of structural thinking: *Cogito ergo sum*.

This early structural tradition in philosophy has had an influence on Western thought. Freud's concept of the unconscious in many ways can be seen as congruent to Plato's World of Ideas. de Shazer and Berg (1992) reflect this:

> ...[The actual words used] can be translated, transformed to, and derived from the underlying deep structure or unconscious and, therefore, the one true meaning of any word is discoverable. (p. 73)

Freud viewed a patient's complaint as a symptom of an underlying, interpsychic conflict. Within this structural orientation, the counselor is viewed as the expert guide. de Shazer et al. (2007) said "This individualistic point of view, with the individual having a special, infallible knowledge of the contents of his or her own mind, is essential to traditional psychology and psychiatry" (p. 103).

Poststructuralism and Meaning

In thinking about this section of the chapter, I first considered writing about the similarities and differences between social constructivism, social constructionism, and postmodernism. In the former Brief Family Therapy Center offices on Capitol Drive in Milwaukee, there was a bumper sticker reading "KISS" ("Keep It Simple, Stupid") above the one-way mirror. For me, this seems like good advice. I decided to write about poststructuralism; for me, it combines elements of the other -isms and yet maintains a certain minimalism.

Geyerhofer and Komori (2004) state:

> de Shazer and Berg were the first to use the term "poststructuralist" to describe those models of therapy that are mainly concerned with what the clients tell the therapist and each other – with the interaction between the "text," the "reader" and the "writer" of those stories constructed in therapy. (p. 47)

de Shazer (personal communication, 1994) used the term poststructuralism descriptively; he stated that it simply places the philosophical foundations as occurring chronologically after structuralism. In describing poststructuralism, he incorporates the philosophy of Wittgenstein and certainly infers that post-structuralism offers an alternative to structuralist thinking.

While structuralism views meanings as fixed, poststructuralism views meanings as "known through social interaction and negotiating" (de Shazer, 1991, p. 45). One might characterize a structural conversation as discovering meanings. Conversely, one might characterize a poststructural conversation as inventing meanings or as Berg and de Shazer (1993) state, "There is yet another view, which is usually labeled *poststructuralism*, that suggests, simply, that language *is* reality" (p. 7).

Wittgenstein (1958) states, "For a *large* class of cases – though not for all – in which we employ the word 'meaning' it can be defined thus: the meaning of the word is its use in the language" (p. 20). For Wittgenstein, the words themselves are meaningless outside the context of language; "This was what Frege meant, too, when he said that a word has meaning only as part of a sentence" (p. 24).

Knowledge follows language and language, in turn, functions in social contexts. Knowing is not an isolated, internal activity but an activity that people do together. We use language in social contexts (Gergen, 1985).

Our sense of what is real results from the co-constructed meanings of the words that are used in conversations with others. These meanings are applicable only in the context of the conversation. Once the context changes – time, place, and participants – there will be new meanings to be renegotiated (Simon & Berg, 2004). The words we use have meanings that are only specific to their conversational contexts. Our sense of what is real is constantly shifting.

Anderson and Goolishian (1992) state that the clinician "is always on the way to co-understanding with clients, but never understands" (p. 13). As clients co-construct newer (and hopefully more useful) meanings for themselves, their perspectives will change accordingly. As clinicians engage clients in conversations about what they understand, new meanings emerge. As clients go through their daily lives, they have myriads of conversations with other people. Each new conversation creates new opportunities for co-constructing different meanings. Poststructural conversations can be described as a system of meaning-making, open feedback loops.

Chapter 3 Use of Language in Solution Focus

This process can have consequences whether the client and clinician engage in problem talk or in solution talk. Both will have consequences for what the client does based upon how he co-constructs his situation, himself, and others. The more the client and therapist explore the problem, the more they together co-construct the problem. The more they describe exceptions, resources, and desired futures, the more these become real (Berg & de Shazer, 1993).

In my training sessions, I use an exercise that divides the training group into two smaller subgroups (Simon, 2005). Each group is given an identical case history; the only difference is the instructions. One group is instructed to view the case from a traditional case conference perspective: problem exploration, diagnosis and prognosis without intervention. The other group is told to predict a positive outcome based upon the client's personal and social resources.

The results of the exercise are very instructive and parallel this concept of co-constructing what is "real." As would be expected, the former group returns with a problem-saturated picture and a very poor prognosis. The latter group returns with a much more optimistic result and has creatively described the client as a success. I then pose the question, armed with their respective assumptions, "What will be the likely conversations with the client in both the first and last case? Finally, what will be the most likely result for the client based upon those conversations?"

Returning to our hypothetical Elizabeth, let us suppose that the clinician has a very different conversation with her. The focus of the conversation is on her strengths and resources, and the results of employing those strengths and resources. Instead of theorizing this as a problem in differentiation, perhaps Elizabeth might be told that her reactions are a normal part of the grieving process. The clinician then might continue to find out from Elizabeth how she will know that she is beginning to move beyond her grief, and then instructs Elizabeth to spend some time looking for signs of healing in her life. It is very likely that the results of this conversation will be very different.

A poststructural conversation diverges from a traditional focus on the deeper meaning of the grief experience to co-constructing an alternative sense of what is real. Goolishian and Anderson (1992) summarize this concept: "Therapeutic conversation is the process through which the therapist and the client participate in the co-development of new meanings, new realities, and new narratives" (p. 12).

LANGUAGE-GAMES

Ever since I was introduced to the concept of "language-game," I have found it a very useful way of thinking about what happens in conversations. The concept of language-game was first introduced and described by Wittgenstein (1958):

> We can also think of the whole process of using words as one of those games by means of which children learn their native language. I will call these games "language-games" and will sometimes speak of a primitive language as a language-game.
>
> And the process of naming the stones and of repeating words after someone might also be called language-games. Think of much of the use of words in games like ring-a-ring-a-roses.
>
> I shall also call the whole, consisting of language and the actions into which it is woven, the "language-game." (p. 5)

de Shazer et al. (2007) describe language-games as "everyday practices and activities in which words are used that provide words with their meaning" (p. 110).

Simon and Nelson (2007) state:

> All of social interaction involves language-games. Language-games are the rules and grammar of different kinds of conversations and are the only tools we have for knowing about others' realities. (p. 165)

We are trained to be in various language-games and therefore they are experienced by us as being natural and as a part of everyday life. Wittgenstein (op. cit.) states, "Here the teaching of language is not explanation, but training" (p. 4).

It may be helpful to use the games of checkers and chess as an example of language-game. Both games share elements of play that include:

- The field of play is a square consisting of 64 squares (eight rows and columns) of alternating colors.
- "Pieces" are moved on the board as part of the play.
- The pieces of one side are of a different color than the pieces of the other side.
- Players take turns moving the pieces.
- There are rules that govern how the pieces are moved.
- There is a defined winner and defined loser.

But just as there are commonalities there are also differences that include:

- The checker pieces are flat; chess pieces are varied.
- The pieces in checkers are arranged initially on the board very differently from the pieces of chess.
- The movement of checker pieces is very different than the movements of chess pieces.
- The object of checkers (the defined end of the game and therefore defined winner and loser) is to capture all the opponent's pieces by jumping over them. The object of chess is to place the one piece called the "king" in a situation where it is liable for capture and no matter where it might move would likewise be liable for capture.

We can therefore state that the language-game of checkers has some similarities and differences to the chess language-game. If one were to attempt to act in the rules of a checker language-game while playing a game of chess, the opponent might express some confusion. Likewise, if one were to act in a language-game normally reserved for cocktail parties at a funeral, the gathered mourners might express both confusion, consternation, and there is very good probability that the offender might be subject to social censorship.

I am reminded of an incident that occurred relatively early in my solution focused career that may further help to illustrate this point. I was asked to present a workshop for consumers (as they were called in those days), families of consumers, consumer advocates, and professional staff at the state psychiatric center that had been located in the county where I live and work. My chosen topic was "Solution-Building Conversations." Before I could say a word, a consumer advocate began to assail me. As I could best ascertain from her comments, which tended to be rather rambling and disjointed, she was accusing me of being one of the many minions of professionals who perpetuate the mythology of psychiatric illness and, as such, prevent consumers from realizing their full potentials.

When I could get in a word or two, I attempted to explain that what I was planning to present would be more supportive of her point of view rather than opposed. This seemed to fall on deaf ears as she continued haranguing me. I finally suggested that we exchange places and, since she was more determined than I to get her message across, I would listen. She refused. This finally ended when one of the social workers spoke up, said that he had come to hear what I had to say, and that perhaps the advocate might give me a chance to present my ideas. The advocate left the room.

As I was thinking about this section on language-games, I was reminded of this incident and thought that it might illustrate what happens when noncomplimentary language-games occur. The advocate was clearly in her advocacy language-game; I was clearly in a very different language-game. Her behaviors, feelings, and thoughts were very consistent within her language-game – as were mine. I was in a teaching language-game; she was certainly not in a complementary language-game. We both were not very successful inviting the other into our respective or complementary language-games. The aforementioned social worker, who intervened, did so from a desire to engage in a language-game complementary to my teaching one. The advocate at this point could have chosen to be in a different language-game or leave – she left.

Wittgenstein's phrase cited above, "I shall also call the whole, consisting of language and the actions into which it is woven, the 'language-game,' is instructive." The suggestion is that language and action are interwoven. Therein lies the power of co-constructive conversations; what takes place between the client and the clinician is the making of word meanings and the resultant action that inevitably follows. The clinician endeavors to provide the context in which more useful meanings and, therefore, actions can occur. Cantwell and Holmes (1994) state: "The task of the therapist is to be a midwife for new meanings to arise" (p. 18). Goolishian and Anderson (1992) expand on this concept:

> The therapist's role, expertise, and emphasis in this conversational process is to develop a free and open conversational space and to facilitate an emerging dialogical process in which "newness" can occur. The emphasis, for the therapist, is not on producing change, but on opening space for conversation. (p. 13)

THE ROLE OF EMOTIONS IN COUNSELING

Isabel's mother died two months prior to her meeting with me for bereavement counseling. After a few preliminary questions, I asked her how she would know that our conversation together was helpful to her. Isabel replied that she was in a "deep depression" and desperately needed to "get the feelings out."

Chapter 3 Use of Language in Solution Focus

Isabel's statement of goal is not unusual; I hear similar statements frequently, whether it is "getting the feelings out," or "venting." Freud and Breuer developed the "cathartic method" of psychotherapy that would later become the root of Psychoanalysis (and a major characteristic of popular psychology) (Brill, 1938). Ever since, feelings have come under intense scrutiny and have become the province of counseling.

In Freud's essay entitled *The Sexual Aberrations* in the same text, he states:

> There is only one way to obtain a thorough and unerring solution of problems in the sexual life of so-called psychoneurotics (hysteria, obsessions, the wrongly named neurasthenia, and surely also dementia praecox and paranoia), and that is by subjecting them to that cathartic or psychoanalytic investigation, discovered by J. Breuer and me. (p. 573)

Ever since, the focus on emotional expression has become the gold standard for counseling – at least, until challenged by other theories taking a more behavioral approach. Still, for the lay public – especially in the context of bereavement – the concept of catharsis as the route to healing holds great sway.

de Shazer (personal communication, 1999) said that the problem with most theories is that people who hold to them do not take them to their logical conclusions. When the theories are taken to their logical conclusions, their apparent absurdities become evident. Catharsis treats feelings as if they are substances that somehow get in us, take up space within us, and eventually, if there is no release, overwhelm us and compel us to behave, think, and feel in ways that we ordinarily would not. According to this theory, it then becomes the clinician's job to act metaphorically as the valve on a pressure cooker to cause the client to release his or her pent up feelings.

de Shazer (personal communication, 1997) said that you do not read Wittgenstein to find out what he thinks; you read Wittgenstein to find out what *you* think. Wittgenstein (op. cit.) writes, "inner process stands in need of outward criteria" (p. 153). There are two possible meanings I take from this phrase. The first is that any emotion must have a behavioral manifestation that is consistent with what we would expect with anyone claiming to have that emotion. I can say "I am angry" and that statement could not be denied since I am reporting on an internal, subjective feeling. However, in order for me to say, "you are angry," I would need to point to some behavior that would be consistent (Shazer et al., 2007).

There is perhaps another way of understanding Wittgenstein's phrase. Emotions are a matter of training. In some cultures, the language-game of grief involves stoicism. In other cultures, the death of a loved one is met with an outpouring of emotions that include beating one's chest and wailing. Both are appropriate outward expressions of inner processes within the context of their respective culture's language-game.

I believe de Shazer et al. (ibid.) reflect this meaning in their writing:

> Thus, in Wittgenstein's view, the individual does not have special, private knowledge about his or her own inner states and processes. In order for us to talk about, make sense of, and perhaps define, these inner processes, we need outward criteria that can be referenced and shared with others. (p. 34)

Emotional expression can be viewed as part of the training the child receives. The child learns to express feelings by observing what are the appropriate language-games in the appropriate contexts. In some cases, the child may be directly instructed; "We are going to a funeral and it is expected that you dress well, you talk softly, you sit quietly" and so forth.

Much of the muddle comes from focusing on emotions as separate from their contexts. Emotions are part of the fabric of social activity and as such are subject to co-constructive realities. When emotions are studied outside of their social contexts and treated as specialized fields of study, clinical work becomes needlessly complex (Miller & de Shazer, 2000).

In the previous discussion of language, I explored the concept that the meanings of words are their uses in language. Recall also Wittgenstein's agreement with Frege that a word only has meaning as part of a sentence. Logically, the expressions of emotions make sense only as part of the conversational contexts in which the emotions occur. To take emotions out of the conversational context renders them meaningless.

To paraphrase de Shazer's previous statement, talking about problems in effect creates problems. Herein lies another logical inconsistency that regards emotion as the *primeum mobile* of the healing process. The client's focus on the pain makes the pain more real – this is how language functions. How will they (the client and the clinician) know that they've done enough of the cathartic work if, through their conversations, they are actually creating more of the negative affect they seek to alleviate?

4 Principles of Solution Building

> Hereafter, in a better world than this,
> I shall desire more love and knowledge of you.
> —*William Shakespeare,*
> *As You Like It, Act I, Scene 2*

PROBLEM SOLVING vs. SOLUTION BUILDING

Dan Gallagher, Janet Campbell, and I were just about to do a presentation on solution focus. The person introducing us said, "This a group of trainers from Center for Solutions and they're going to be talking to us about solution focused-problem solving." She had made a very common mistake: making meaning of solution focus in a problem-solving language-game. The solution focused language-game is very different from the problem solving language-game.

There are certainly contexts in which problem solving is a useful skill. There have been times that I have noticed that my car is acting abnormally. I freely admit that my knowledge of automobile functioning and repair is elementary, at best. I take my car to my local mechanic because he has proven many times to be an expert at diagnosing and treating the underlying causes of abnormal automotive behaviors.

Likewise, when I am not feeling well and it is evident that a call to my physician is warranted, I want the doctor to do a differential diagnosis and, based upon that diagnosis, prescribe a course of treatment. I want to make clear that this chapter refers specifically to the application of problem solving to emotional and psychological problems.

PROBLEM SOLVING

Generally, problem solving involves these steps:

- Explore the problem
- Hypothesize the etiology or "real cause" of the problem
- Name the problem
- Explore the effect of the problem on the individual
- If necessary, motivate the client to continue the process
- Based upon the above, devise or revise the treatment plan
- Apply the treatment plan in hopes that it will lead to the dissolution of the problem
- If successful, treatment is terminated; if unsuccessful, find the causes and solve

Problem Exploration

In the problem-solving language-game, the complaints that clients bring to bear are assumed to have underlying causes. As in the hypothetical example of Elizabeth in Chapter 3, the clinician theorized that Elizabeth's reaction to her mother's death was only a symptom of an underlying, interpsychic conflict. A failure to completely separate/individuate was the real cause – her grief was the effect. Information is the fodder of problem solving. Within this language-game, the belief is that the more information the clinician can gather, the greater the chance of discovering the solution.

Naming the Problem

Once sufficient information has been gathered, the problem can then be named. In a more clinical context, this would be the client's diagnosis.

While doing a search of literature on diagnosis, I was not surprised by the volume of references to diagnostic methodology. I was surprised by how little appears to be written about the purposes of diagnosis. In his article entitled "On the Ethics of Constructing Realities," Harry Korman (www.sikt.nu, 1997) addresses the topic of the supposed function of diagnosis:

> The purpose of the classification thus created is for the physician/therapist to know what to do. There is a basic belief that from the way we group "symptoms" together and call them something, hysteria, neurosis, schizophrenia, alcoholism, enmeshed families, etc., will emerge knowledge of specific treatments, psychological or biological, that will be tailored for the underlying condition causing the specific "illness" thus named.... The behaviors thus classified will always be indicative of an "underlying" problem, disturbance, or disease. "Deviant" behavior will always have underlying causes[;] individual, contextual, biological or different combinations of these and finding these causes is essential for treatment. (p. 1)

In the context of problem solving, diagnosis is a prerequisite to the treatment plan.

Explore the Effect of the Problem on the Individual

Once the client has been assigned a diagnosis, it then becomes necessary to track the problem in his or her everyday life. It is theorized that this process will lead to a greater insight into the underlying causes that have resulted in the symptoms. Different theories will have different explanations for the exploration. The psychoanalyst's theory suggests that the patient must come to understand the interpsychic conflicts that are the "true causes" of the problem. The client working with the cognitive behavioral therapist is directed to become aware of the cognitive distortions that are his or her "true causes." In either case, the inferred directive for the client is to become more aware of the "real" problem from the clinician's preferred Theoretical orientation.

The additional information about the problem that the client gathers between clinical contacts is then brought back into the consulting room. The clinician then uses this information and his or her expertise to help the client develop greater insight into the problem and, more importantly, its underlying cause.

If Necessary, Motivate

The process of problem exploration is a long and tedious one and may often leave the client with a sense of dissatisfaction and despair. It may become necessary at these times to convince the client to stay the course. Different clinicians and different theoretical orientations may have different ways of doing this. One strategy is to explain to the client the relevant theoretical concepts.

For example, the clinician might frame the client's response as a function of resistance and then the goal becomes helping the client to "work through" his or her resistance. Alternatively, the clinician may explain that such feelings are often an important part of the process and it will probably be necessary for "things to get worse before they get better." As a last resort, the clinician could warn the client of the dire consequences should he or she refuse to continue with treatment.

Devise or Revise the Treatment Plan

During the process, the client may discover something significantly new about his or her past, the problem may arise in a totally different arena, or the problem may arise in a totally different way. As the client continues the process, new information may require a revision of the hypotheses as to the "real" cause of the problem. As the clinician and client come closer to understanding the "true" cause of the problem, the interventions necessary for the resolution of the problem should also become clearer.

Apply the Treatment Plan

As the interventions are applied, the clinician needs to assess whether or not they will have the desired effect. They may not necessarily result in an alleviation of the symptoms, although ultimately that is what is hoped for by the both client and the clinician. If the symptoms do remediate too soon in the treatment process (according to the clinician/expert), the clinician will often express skepticism. Premature improvement might be viewed, for example, as a "flight into health," meaning that the improvements are likely temporary and superficial. Especially in the beginning and middle stages of treatment, successful interventions should result in an even greater understanding of the problem and not usually a cessation of symptoms.

Success or a Lack of Success

It is assumed that the clinician – an expert on such matters with training, experience, and expertise – will devise a treatment plan that will have a beneficial result. There may be several reasons why the client's situation has not improved: client resistance, client noncompliance to the treatment recommendations, or client denial, just to name a few. In my experience, the usual assumption is that the reason for a lack of progress is clearly the province of the client, and not the clinician's theoretical orientation or interventional techniques. Another major reason for a lack of success may be insufficient or inaccurate information.

If the causes are the former, the treatment plan will be revised to help the client gain insight into his or her resistance, denial, noncompliance, etc. If the latter, the problem-solving process will need to begin again, new and/or additional information must be attained, and new (perhaps more accurate) insights gained.

Information satiates the hunger of problem solving. In order for the problem-solving process to go forth, the problem must be constructed as constant and unwavering. Exceptions have to be viewed as irrelevant, for no real solution can occur without an exhaustive exploration and an in-depth processing of the problem. Ultimately, the goal of the problem-solving process is to find the one solution that fits and solves the problem.

SOLUTION BUILDING

Marty's wife of 42 years died six months prior to his first session with a bereavement counselor. When the counselor addressed Marty's goal for their work together, Marty responded, "Most of the time, I'm sad and crying when I think about my wife and how she suffered during the last days of her life. I felt impotent because I couldn't help her."

The clinician had several choices of interventions: sadness, crying, and thoughts about his wife's suffering. The problem-solving clinician is going to naturally be drawn to Marty's sense of sadness and image of his dying wife. However, there is also the temporal statement, "Most of the time." The phrase "most of the time" implies that there are some times when something other than crying, sadness, and thinking about her suffering is happening. The clinician does have the option to ask Marty about those other times.

Bavelas et al. (2000) define formulation as "One of the most common and apparently neutral communicative techniques of the therapist is to summarize or paraphrase what the client has just said" (p. 12).

They continue to say that even though formulations are meant to be neutral, by their very nature they "serve three functions: They *preserve, delete,* and *transform* the original statement" (p. 12). By asking about Marty's sadness, crying, or image of his wife's suffering, the clinician preserves and transforms these elements, yet deletes Marty's introductory phrase "most of the time." The opposite happens when the exceptions inherent within the phrase "most of the time" are addressed. The problem formulations are essentially deleted and the temporal is transformed.

The basics of solution building essentially involve inquiry about exceptions. These may be exceptions in the past, present, or future. The clinician co-constructs the meaning of exceptions by asking about exceptions, and how the exceptions made, make, or will make a difference to the client and others in the client's life. Further, the clinician might ask what the result will be if the exceptions continue to happen or, perhaps, happen even more.

While problem solving seeks *THE* solution to the problem, solution building works with clients to co-construct *A* useful solution. Problem solving logically requires a problem or set of problems that need a solution. Solution building is not dependent upon a problem – all that is required is that the client has a vision of how his or her life might be different and more satisfying.

This is especially applicable to clients who are facing end-of-life and their significant others. Dying is not in and of itself a problem and it is not useful to co-construct the process as such. What meaning the client makes of his or her past and current situation, how he or she chooses to enter this final phase of life, and what remains to be completed are all possible foci.

However, if the client expresses contentment, it is not the clinician's responsibility to co-construct a problem to be resolved. Solution-building questions can address what helped the client reach this stage, what his family and friends do that help him or her maintain this sense of life satisfaction, and in what ways he or she makes useful meaning of his or her life. By so doing, the clinician helps to validate and further co-construct the client's acceptance.

The following are two depictions (admittedly over-simplified) that might help to demonstrate the difference between solution building and problem solving.

Chapter 4 Principles of Solution Building   **57**

SOLUTION FOCUS STANCE

Successful utilization of the solution focus technique requires that the practitioner adopts an attitude of respect for clients. This is not to imply that other practices do not require similar orientations. A clinician, no matter how he or she practices, will hardly be successful if the client does not feel respected and listened to.

The clinician needs steadfastly to assume that *possibilities exist,* even in the direst of situations. This does not mean that solution focused practitioners are pollyannaish and are blind to the emotional and physical pain that individuals facing terminal illnesses experience. It does mean, however, that while the pain is acknowledged, we hold forth the very possibility that change is possible and even inevitable.

Even when the client experiences an overwhelming sense of chaos and turmoil, the clinician strives to co-construct with the client even the smallest area within the client's *control.* We have come to learn by observing and listening to clients that control in one area tends to extend into other areas of clients' lives.

The solution focused clinician respects the *client's version of reality* and realizes that the client and the clinician can be successful together only if the clinician has the flexibility to accept the client and what he or she says is true. The clinical task requires that the clinician cooperates with the client. No matter what the client states, it is best to assume that it is useful and the task is to co-construct its usefulness.

The questions that are asked should be driven by the clinician's (and perhaps the client's) *curiosity.* When I first was trained, I was taught that the clinician asks clients questions with a reasonable certainty about what will be the probable response. This process served to aid the client in further understanding the underlying cause and effect of the presenting problem. As the clinical expert, I could hypothesize what were the client's interpsychic motivations. My role was to guide the client into this realization.

I realized that I had accepted the solution focused language-game when I began to ask questions to which only the client would know the answers and, further, I became curious about how the client would respond. When we become truly curious about clients and, specifically, their strengths and resources, they then sense that we respect them and their experiences, and that we acknowledge that what they have to tell us is important and of value.

Finally, we take a *"not-knowing"* stance as described by Anderson and Goolishian (1992):

> That is, the therapist's actions and attitudes express a need to know more about what has been said rather than convey preconceived opinions and expectations about the client, the problem, or what must be changed. The therapist, therefore, positions himself or herself in such a way as always to be in the state of 'being informed' by the client. (p. 29)

SOLUTION FOCUSED ASSUMPTIONS

Imagine what life would be if we did not assume gravity. We would wake up in the morning and perhaps our first thought might involve there concern of what will happen if we try to put our feet on the ground. It would be virtually impossible to get through the day, wondering with every step whether we might just rise into the air.

The many assumptions that we act upon on a day-to-day basis help facilitate our lives. They allow us to go through life and not have to think each moment of each day whether our feet will stay on the sidewalk, whether we have to take a breath, whether our hearts will continue beating, whether the person next to us will behave in a rational manner, and so many other assumptions.

While it is possible to do counseling without having a Theory, I would contend that every intervention reflects assumptions that clinicians make about themselves, the client, the clinician's role, the client's role, and the respective complementary processes in which both the clinician and the client are mutually engaged.

There are several assumptions that are part of the solution focused language-game [Berg & Miller (1992), Simon & Berg (2004), Simon & Nelson (2007), Thomas & Nelson (2007), Walter & Peller (1992)]:

- It is not necessary to problem solve in order to solution build
- Change is inevitable
- Small changes lead to bigger ones
- One small area of control tends to lead to other areas of control
- People have the resources necessary
- People are experts on themselves
- We are all part of social systems

- Every problem has at least one exception
- Every one of the client's responses is useful
- People are invested in solutions that they create
- Everyone does the best that they can

It Is Not Necessary to Problem Solve in Order to Solution Build

It may seem counterintuitive, but my own experiences, after 17 years of practicing solution focus and after working with many clients in varied settings, strongly suggest that clients need not explore more about the details of problems in order to find a satisfactory solution to the problems they are experiencing. I would suggest that in the context of clinical work, problem solving co-constructs a problem complexity that serves to delay and may even prevent resolution. The language-game of problem solving is very different than the language-game of solution building (see Chapter 3).

Change Is Inevitable

The Greek philosopher Heraclitus, who lived around the fifth or sixth century B.C., stated, "One cannot step into the same river twice" (Jones, 1969, p. 7). The only thing that is inevitable in life is change. Clients often talk about their issues as if they were constant. While clients may perceive their problems as being unchanging, given the nature of change and its inevitability, such perceptions can only be illusionary and therefore subject to deconstruction.

de Shazer (1988) explains the concept of deconstruction:

> Developing some doubt about the global frames involves a process that can best be called deconstructing the frame. During the interview, first as the therapist helps the client search for exceptions, and then as the therapist helps the client imagine a future without the complaint, the therapist is implicitly breaking down the frame into smaller and smaller pieces. As it becomes clearer and clearer that a global frame is involved, the therapist helps the client break it down further into its component parts. The purpose of breaking the frame down is threefold:
>
> 1. The therapist is showing his acceptance of the client by listening closely and carefully asking questions,
> 2. The therapist is attempting to introduce some doubt about the global frame, and

3. The therapist is searching for a piece of the frame's construction upon which a solution can be built. (p. 102)

The solution focused clinician not only accepts the assumption that change is inevitable, he or she also assumes that one of the purposes for interventions is to help the client also realize this frame of reference. If the client's sense of *status quo* is deconstructed, then this opens a world of possibilities that the client did not previously realize.

In their book, *Change: Principles of Problem Formation and Problem Resolution* (Watzlawick et al., 1974), the authors distinguish between first order and second order change. First order change is change that makes no difference. Very often, before clients make an appointment to see a clinician for bereavement, they may have already told their story to any number of people. While this may have provided some momentary relief, such conversations may not ultimately serve to change the client's perception of the problem. Essentially, this is first order change: a change that does not make a difference. If the clinician's theoretical stance suggests that problem solving requires further elucidation by the client about his experiences of the problem, then the clinician is engaging in first order change.

Second order change is a change that actually results in the client thinking, feeling, and/or behaving differently. Helping the client realize that change is not only possible, but also probable, is one potentially powerful second order change intervention.

Small Changes Lead to Bigger Changes

Many clinicians believe that complex problems require complex solutions. Further, it is necessary to gather as much information about the problem in order to effectively help the client. This serves to co-construct an approach that is complex and interminable. When the solution is viewed as separate and independent from the problem, intervention can very much become brief and enduring (de Shazer, 1985).

In Chapter 3, I presented the concept that our sense of what is real is a function of the conversations we have with others and how those conversations make meaning of the words that are used. By assuming that problems and solutions are complex, and by inviting clients into this language-game, the clinician is actually creating the very complexity that he or she seeks to resolve.

By helping clients deconstruct complexity, and by holding out for even the smallest change, the clinician can help open the possibilities for second order change. Once the client experiences a change in the way he or she thinks and/or feels about the problem, the client will naturally act differently as well, not only with the clinician but (more importantly) within his social context. This, in turn, will lead to new conversations, new perceptions, new feelings, and, inevitably, new behaviors. However, change is not only the result of different thoughts and feelings; new behaviors can also change how one thinks and feels. When viewed this way, the mechanism for bigger change from smaller ones becomes evident.

If one accepts the assumption that small changes lead to bigger ones, it would naturally follow that it does not matter where the clinician and the client begin; all that is required is that there is a small change that will make a difference for the client. This has been a thought that has served me well many times.

I received a phone call from a father concerned about his son. His wife, the son's mother, died recently and the son is mourning her loss. In addition, the son has a substance misuse problem, he is having difficulty in school, and there is an ongoing conflict with his older brother that required the police's intervention. Naturally, my first thought was to wonder – with some trepidation – where to begin in a family with such complex problems. I've learned to take a breath and tell myself that it does not matter where I begin; all I need do is help the client take the first small step in a useful direction. Solving complex problems begins with small solutions.

de Shazer (1985) wrote:

> One major difference between brief therapy and other models lies in the brief therapist's idea that no matter how awful and how complex the situation, a small change in one person's behavior can make profound and far-reaching differences in the behavior of all persons involved. (p. 16)

One Small Area of Control Tends to Lead to Other Areas of Control

Clients come to see clinicians basically because they feel overwhelmed and are unsure what is to be done to alleviate the intrusive feelings and thoughts they experience as a result of a loss or from facing a terminal illness themselves or of a significant other. Clients usually have attempted many different ways of seeking relief and many, if not most, involve talking about their feelings to anyone who will listen. This, of course, only serves to increase their despair, their perception of problem constancy, and, therefore, their perception that their world is spinning out of control. The clients perceive this lack of control as a crisis that necessitates professional intervention.

Inherent within crisis is an opportunity for change and very often the individual is more open to intervention. A person in crisis reaches out for something that will give them even the smallest perception of control. Co-constructing and validating exceptions, personal resources, and social resources facilitates the client's perception of control. Once the person experiences this sense of control, this opens them to other areas for control over their life.

People Have the Resources Necessary

Robert was dedicated to his wife, Helen, of 45 years. In the last years of her life, she had become a virtual recluse and Robert was her sole connection to the outside world. This served to increase her dependence upon him and his upon her. When Helen was diagnosed with stage 4 breast cancer, Robert was determined to keep her alive as long as possible; he could not imagine life without her.

Through the six months that Helen remained alive and continued to grow weaker, Robert was dedicated to her care. He left the home only briefly to buy food or supplies but rushed back to care for his wife. The hospice staff that helped care for Helen predicted that Robert would be "lost" without her. They expressed concern that he did not have the personal resiliency and the social resources that would tide him over and help him heal from his loss.

I went to see Robert for bereavement counseling after Helen died. Robert was understandably saddened and expressed a profound lack of direction. I expressed that this made perfect sense to me since he had just spent the past six months focused on caring for Helen. As Robert continued to talk, he spoke about how he had spent the past few days walking through his village on several errands – routine tasks he had been neglecting for quite a while. Everywhere he went, neighbors greeted him and expressed their condolences. They talked about their own memories of Helen and Robert found this comforting.

I returned a week later and Robert related how these experiences were so helpful to him and that he realized how much support he had. He began to talk to me about his plans for the future: becoming active in the church again, continuing the garden that his wife lovingly cared for over the years, putting the house back in order, and reading his bible.

He talked about how much he dearly missed his wife, yet was able to find moments of peace and comfort.

Robert called upon resources within his community and within himself that perhaps even he did not know existed until they were needed. Many times I have been surprised by people's capacity to find the resources necessary in the dire of circumstances. I have learned that it is best that I approach those with whom I work with the assumption that they have the resources, and our job together is to help them to discover and utilize them.

People Are Experts on Themselves

I have been fortunate to sit behind the one-way mirror on several occasions watching Insoo Kim Berg work with clients. In one particular session, Insoo was working with a client referred by his probation officer. The client was talking about a series of behaviors that the probation officer felt he needed insight into to prevent such actions from happening again. Once he had finished describing what he had done, Insoo responded, "You must have had a good reason for doing that."

I had a client who had come to me after her mother had died. I asked her the Miracle Question and after thinking for a while, she replied that she would stop drinking. She continued that she often goes out to one of her friends' house and they play video games and drink beer. It was clear from her description that being with friends was a source of comfort for her and I asked whether that would mean that she would not be with her friends anymore. She replied that she could still be with her friends but learn to limit her drinking.

Both Insoo and I were operating from the same assumption: the client is an expert on him or herself. The client's behaviors, thoughts, and feelings make sense only within the social contexts of those behaviors, thoughts, and feelings. It is presumptuous of the clinician to believe that he or she knows more about clients' lives than clients know about themselves. A corollary to this assumption is the idea that since the clinician can only helpfully misunderstand the client, it is required that the clinician takes what the client says at face value.

We Are All Part of Social Systems

Many theoretical approaches prescribe that the focus of therapy should be on the relationship between the clinician and the client. Freud (Brill,

1938), in his essay on the "History of Psychoanalysis," stated that transference and resistance – both reflective of the relationship between the clinician and client – solely define the practice of psychoanalysis.

Solution focused practice takes a very different stance; the focus is on what happens in people's lives beyond the contact with the clinician that makes a positive difference. While many approaches emphasize the relationship between the clinician and the client as a major curative factor, solution focus emphasizes what happens in the client's life outside of the clinician's office that would change his or her life for the better. The fact remains that all clients spend a greater majority of their time and have the greater amount of experiences outside of the clinician's office (Simon & Nelson, 2007).

Quoting Watzlawick, de Shazer (1985) describes "a system is a whole, every part of a system is so related to its fellow parts that change in one part will cause a change in all of them and in the total system" (p. 105). We all live, work, and play in social systems. Sometimes for better and sometimes for worse, we affect and are affected by those very systems in which we participate. If we focus solely on what happens between the clinician and the client, we are neglecting a major part of the client's life where the potential for change takes place hour-by-hour and day-by-day. We also miss a chance to deconstruct the notion that the problem is constant and unchanging. Ultimately, the possibilities for change are directly proportionate to the number of social contacts.

Every Problem Has at Least One Exception

Not soon after I started working at Hospice of Orange and Sullivan Counties, I was asked to present on solution building at the annual all-staff training day. After presenting the concepts, I asked whether there were any questions. In reference to a statement that problems have exceptions, one of the social workers asked me, "What if the problem is dying?"

de Shazer (1991) states that the concept of "problem" has (as with most concepts) both an "inside" – that which belongs to the problem – and an "outside" – the exceptions to the problem. By definition, problems are defined by their exceptions. The exceptions hold keys to solutions. What we suppose is a "problem," which does not imply an exception, is not a problem. "Problems" without exceptions are not problems at all; they are a fact of life (Berg, personal communication).

I responded to the aforementioned social worker that death in and of itself is not a problem (since there are no exceptions) and, therefore, it would be a futile endeavor to attempt to co-construct a solution to that which is a fact of life. However, how the client and family cope with end-of-life issues and how they wish to usefully experience this phase of their life together are all goals that can possibly be co-constructed.

This concept is also relevant to those experiencing feelings of loss due to the death of a significant other. While it makes perfect sense that someone would view the problem as the loss, that loss *per se* has no exception and therefore its co-construction would not lead in a useful direction. When the clinician, by asking thoughtful and respectful questions, helps the client to explore life after the loss, for example, there is a higher probability that their work together will result in something beneficial for the client.

Every One of the Client's Responses Is Useful

I have found it beneficial to assume that the client is being cooperative and that my job is to cooperate with the client. Counseling proceeds much more smoothly if we begin with that assumption. It then follows that the clinician's job is to best determine how to use the client's responses in a way that will both create a bond with and ultimately benefit the client. The alternative is to misunderstand the client as being "resistant" and then to expend a tremendous amount of time and energy attempting to convince the client to think as we do.

In the article, "Brief Therapy: Focused Solution Development," de Shazer et al. (1986) state:

> We had long been puzzled by the notion of "resistance" in therapy. As we watched each other work, we became more and more convinced that clients really do want to change. Certainly some of them found that our idea about how to change did not fit very well. Rather than seeing this as "resistance," however, we viewed it more as the clients' way of letting us know how to help them. (p. 209)

People Are Invested in Solutions They Create

There is an adage that advice is something easily given but difficult to take. The difficulty with advice giving is that it is given within the clinician's life context, and too often there is little fit between the advice and the client's life. Because of the complexity of problems and the often crisis nature of end-of-care and bereavement work, it is very tempting for clinicians to advise clients and families about what they should and should not do. Sometimes this works because clients and families in crisis may be more amenable to such intervention. However, it often serves only to delay action.

In Chapter 3, the concept of language-game was explored. Recall that all language-games consist of the whole of language and *actions*. When we invite clients into solution building language-games, we allow them to be experts on their own lives and then help them co-construct useful directions that are congruent to their lives. This increases the probability that they will do something that will make a difference.

It might seem that the shortest route to change is by telling clients what they should or should not do. The problem with this formula is that it leaves out a crucial component: the client. When the client decides that the advice does not suit them, the temptation for the clinician is to frame this as resistance or denial. This then requires that the resistance be confronted and worked through. This may lead to a disconnect between the clinician and the client, which then needs to be repaired before the process can go ahead. In fact, the faster route is to engage clients in conversations that respect their experiences and ideas and helps them to formulate useful action. Insoo Kim Berg once said (personal communication) that "brief therapy goes slowly."

Everyone Does the Best They Can

Milton Erickson viewed symptoms that clients described as solutions that had worked at one time but no longer served their original purpose, and have become habitual (O'Hanlon, 1987). Life can be complicated, at times, and events happen to all of us that are beyond our control. We then struggle to gain some sense of stability and balance.

I have often told clients – tongue firmly planted in cheek – that there are three very complicated principles of life: 1) If it isn't broken, don't fix it. 2) If it's working, do more of it. 3) If it isn't working, stop and do something different (Berg & Miller, 1992). When we acknowledge our trust that the client is doing the best he or she can and then help him or her do what is working (or find alternatives to that which is not), we help the client take the first meaningful steps toward greater control over his or her own life. As was previously written, one small area of control tends to grow into others.

BRIEF VS. SHORT-TERM COUNSELING

The terms "brief" and "short term" have often been used interchangeably in reference to counseling. I have often heard solution focus referred to as short-term therapy. In practice, there is a difference between "brief" and "short term."

The focus of short-term counseling is on the limits of time. Most often, short-term counselors will inform the client that their contact is bound by a specific number of sessions. Many counselors work purposefully from a short-term approach believing that the element of time will motivate the client. Other counselors work short-term because they are so required by the constraints, for example, of managed care.

de Shazer (personal communication, 1997) reported on research that was done at BFTC. Fifty clients were randomly assigned to one of two different groups. In the first group, the clients were told that they had a maximum of 20 sessions; the second group was told there were a maximum of 10 sessions. There was little or no progress in the first group until about session 17 or 18. Likewise, the second group evidenced little progress until session 8 or 9.

In the introduction to Yvonne Dolan's book (1991), *Resolving Sexual Abuse: Solution Focused Therapy and Ericksonian Hypnosis for Adult Survivors,* de Shazer expressed how most solution-focused practitioners define "brief." He said that brief means taking as many sessions as necessary to develop a satisfactory solution to the problem that motivated the client to see a counselor.

In solution focus, the emphasis is on developing a useful goal and it is the achievement of the goal (or at least an approximation that is satisfactory to the client) that dictates when clinical services are no longer needed. In hospice work, where social work contact, for example, is dictated by regulation and agency policy, the clinician needs to be clear whether the visits with a dying patient and the family are based upon the client's and family's goals or whether it is based upon regulatory requirements.

In the case of the latter, a solution focused approach can be helpful in affirming what the family does that is helpful to the client and what the client does to help him- or herself. In addition, the clinician can help the family members realize their need to create a respite from care giving so that they can return fresher and more capable of coping with the demanding care of a significant other facing end-of-life. One of the benefits of the solution focused approach is that a defined problem is not necessary for practice.

In one such case, I had accompanied a social worker on a routine visit to a wife and grown son who were caring for a patient in the final days of his life. As is often the case, the patient was exhibiting restless behaviors and required almost constant care. Initially, the son expressed that he was understandably exhausted. I asked him for the details of what he does that is helpful to his father and how he knows that it is helpful.

I then asked him what he does that allows him to continue to care as well as he does. He talked about the times he is able to take a break even for a few moments and how these precious moments make a difference. As we departed, the son expressed appreciation for the visit and remarked that the conversation had been very helpful to him. The social worker, new to solution focus at the time, remarked to me that initially he could not figure out how to adapt the solution focus approach in work with dying patients and their families. However, after participating in the session, the social worker discovered that it could indeed be done very naturally with beneficial results.

One of the long-standing mythologies is that longer-term counseling yields more complete and longer-lasting results. One of the common criticisms of solution focus (and brief counseling in general) is that because it is brief, the results are inferior. In a review of the research on brief therapy in general, Koss and Butcher (*Handbook of Psychotherapy and Behavior Change*, Garfield & Bergin, eds., 1986) state:

> Most psychotherapeutic contacts, whether by plan or by premature termination, are brief, lasting less than eight sessions.... Comparative studies of brief and unlimited therapies show essentially no differences in results. (p. 662)

While on the subject of brief, I would be remiss not to mention the purposeful placement of the word in solution focused *brief* practice. I have sometimes heard the approach referred to as brief solution focus. de Shazer (personal communication) stated that the original intention of BFTC was not to develop a brief approach *per se* – the interest was in researching effective therapy. What they found was that as they were more effective, the practice became briefer. It is solution focused brief practice because brief results from working solution focused.

CO-CONSTRUCTING GOALS WITH CLIENTS

The emphasis of solution focused brief practice is on co-constructing a useful goal with the client. It is the goal that is the determinate of whether further clinical intervention is necessary

The dictionary (Abate, ed., 1997) defines goal as: "1. Object of a person's ambition or effort; destination; aim." Goals are always dynamic; the stated differences that clients co-construct with clinicians may, and usually do, change over time as clients live their lives. Perhaps a more accurate phrase for what the client and I attempt to achieve is a "sense of direction" rather than a goal.

Together the clinician and the client strive to co-construct and validate progress so that the client is reasonably confident that he or she can continue without further clinical intervention. To a large extent, discussion around this sense of direction is simply a way of helping the client build solutions and serves to keep practice brief.

Goals that facilitate the clinical process have the following characteristics [Berg & Miller (1992), De Shazer (1991), Simon & Nelson (2007), Thomas & Nelson (2007), Walter & Peller (1992)]:

- Important to the client
- Possible within the client's life context
- Presence of the difference
- A beginning
- Concrete and measurable
- Has meaning for both the client and the clinician
- Is perceived by the client as involving "hard work"

Important to the Client

Too often in more traditional approaches, it is the clinician, because of his or her expertise, that ultimately decides what the client's goal *really* is. It matters less that the client states a goal that is vaguely formulated since, ultimately, it is the clinician's theoretical stance that will dictate the "true" goals for therapy. In solution focused brief practice, what the client states is the goal, *is* the goal – no more and no less. It is the clinician and client's job together to co-construct how the stated goal will make a difference to the client in his or her life.

I recall a group that I led in a community mental health clinic. The subject of the group was on constructive ways of using anger. One of the group members was an artist. When she was asked how she would know that she was taking the first steps, she replied that she would be organizing her workspace. One of the other group members commented that he could not understand what the relationship was between that and better expression of anger. The woman replied that a more organized workspace would result in more orderly thinking and this, in turn, would yield a greater sense of calmness and peace.

Possible Within the Client's Life Context

It is not the clinician's job to convince the client of what is and is not possible; this is the province of the client. The job of the clinician is to *gently* challenge the client to demonstrate that the goal is possible. I have often found it useful to ask a client, "So, what makes you think that this is possible?" The response is to either provide concrete examples – often in the form of exceptions to the problem – or to revise the goal to something more realistic.

Presence of the Difference

Clients will often initially express the goal in negative terms, "I don't want to be sad," or "I don't want to cry every time I mention my husband's name." By definition, goals can only be stated in positive terms; "negative goal" is a contradiction. When the clinician hears the client utter what he or she does not want to be happening, the clinician should hear the statement as only the first step toward formulating a functional goal. I have found the most useful question to an "I don't want…" statement is to simply ask the client what he or she wants to be thinking, feeling, or doing instead.

A Beginning

Simon and Berg (2004) state:

> Life is about constant change and transformations. Solution focus brief therapists tend to be practical about when therapy has reached a useful end. Solution focus therapists are interested in what will tell clients that they have made a good enough start and can continue the process on their own. (p. 4)

Counseling, no matter how effective it may be, will never eliminate the challenges that we all face in this journey we call life. By helping clients negotiate and achieve practical goals, clinicians ultimately help clients realize and utilize their personal and social resources so that they can face life's challenges with greater confidence.

BFTC (de Shazer, 1991) conducted a random survey of approximately 250 former clients 17 months after their last session. In a prior survey the clients reported a success rate of 80.4%. At the 17-month survey, the clients reported that the success rate had increased to 86 percent. Speculatively, the change could very well have been because the clients gained confidence in their own abilities after coping with other challenges in their lives. Bereavement clients who have engaged in solution focused sessions reported to me that they were more quickly able to heal from experiencing deaths of other significant others.

What helps keep solution focus brief is the idea that counseling is about good enough beginnings (Gallagher, personal communication). Clinical work becomes more complicated and prolonged when the client comes to believe that the power for change resides within the clinician. Conversely, when clients come to realize that the power for change resides within them, clinical work tends to be brief.

Concrete and Measurable

It makes sense that the clearer the client and clinician are about what the client wants to be different, the better the chance that it will be achieved. The best way to achieve such clarity is by asking the client for details of the difference: where it will be happening, when it will be happening, with whom it will be happening, how people will notice the difference, and how the difference will make a difference.

There is, however, another reason why co-constructing concrete and measurable goals will prove beneficial. Once again, the idea that language creates and reinforces our sense of what is real comes into play. By co-constructing the details of the difference with the client, we make achievement of the difference more real. This is why I have heard many clients tell me that they left the first session perceiving that they now have a direction, and this gave them a sense of hope and expectation.

Has Meaning for Both the Client and Clinician

The natural first response to the question, "What do you want to be different?" is the "not" statement ("I don't want to cry when I think about my deceased husband"). The clinician needs to ask him or herself what the statement means. It is likely that if what the client says is vague to the clinician, it is probably vague to the client as well. A goal is only useful if it is possible in the client's life situation, and the details of the difference can be envisioned and articulated by the client. This requires that the client and clinician together co-construct the details of the change. Meanings are negotiated in the conversations we have with the clients. Asking clients about the details of change makes the meanings clearer and more real. The paradox of working briefly is that the greater the details, the greater the possibilities of change.

Is Perceived by the Client as Involving "Hard Work"

It is human nature to hold precious that which we obtain through perseverance and hard work. When the clinician helps the client recognize the hard work that it took to accomplish the goal (either fully or partially), the client comes to value and build on the results (Berg & Miller, 1992).

CUSTOMERSHIP: THE COUNSELING RELATIONSHIP

de Shazer (1988) outlined three possible client/therapist relationships: visitors, complainants and customers. He cautioned, "the 'labels' are solely meant to give the observer a thumbnail description of the relationship between the therapist and her client" (p. 87). Unfortunately, I have heard the terms used as labels, for example, "What do you expect. He's just a visitor." Any label tends to reify the individual that it is applied to, no matter that the label is "borderline" or "visitor." It is a short step from classifying someone a visitor to blaming him or her when insufficient progress is being made.

Within the team I was working at time, we began describing the therapist/client relationship in terms of customership. Our assumption was that clients made the effort to see a clinician for good reasons. The reason may not be that the client perceived that he or she needed to change. The reason might be that someone else (a spouse, a teacher, a parent, a probation officer, another therapist, or the courts) wanted the person to behave in a different way.

We viewed our job to be finding out what the person was a customer for, and then help him or her move in a useful direction. By taking this stance, we helped the client feel respected, and this, in turn, helped us develop a cooperative and collaborative relationship.

5   The Tools of Solution Building

> What's gone and what's past help
> Should be past grief.
> —*William Shakespeare,*
> **The Winter's Tale,** *Act III, Scene 2*

One of the common criticisms of solution focus is that there is an emphasis on intervention techniques. No matter to what Theory the clinician subscribes, the only tools that he or she has in working with clients are the interventions that are used. While the clinician may believe that what he or she says and does with the client is driven from a Theory or a family of related Theories, the fact remains that, ultimately, he or she is using technique. The only question is whether or not the technique helps to evoke second order change.

The tools of solution focus are the questions that we use to help the client deconstruct the current frame and co-construct a more useful one. Since the inception of solution focus brief practice, practitioners have sought ways to tweak the questions to achieve even greater effect.

The questions, however, are only the beginning of a useful conversation. I may have asked the Miracle Question about the same way a thousand times in the past 16 years, but how the client responds and where the conversation goes after that response serves to create a unique fingerprint for that client and the conversation. The first rule of using questions as tools is that the clinician carefully listens and ensures that the next questions follow from the client's responses.

I have had many opportunities to supervise students in Masters of Social Work programs. I have also had the opportunity of observing their practice as part of an observation team behind a one-way mirror or via a video camera. It became clear to me that beginning practitioners of solution focus become so caught up in formulating the next question that they miss the client's responses. Once clinicians become comfortable with the questions, they are able to relax, listen carefully to the client, devise questions that are responsive, and better listen with solution-building ears.

SOLUTION-BUILDING QUESTIONS

A Word About Engagement

Miller et al. (1997) suggested that there are four common curative elements that account for success no matter the theory or model of practice. Citing Lambert (1992), they continue to list these in order of contribution to change: extratherapeutic factors, therapy relationship, model and technique; hope, expectancy, and placebo factors. Of these factors, therapy relationship accounts for only 30 percent of positive change.

Many other systems of clinical practice put an emphasis on practitioner/client engagement. Many of these emphasize that clinical engagement occurs over time and is the *sine qua non* of good practice (Simon & Nelson, 2002). However, the fact that only 30 percent of positive change can be attributed to the clinical relationship calls into question the wisdom of this theory. Further, in terms of the element of time, Miller et al. (op. cit.) state:

> In contrast to what one might expect, the research does not show that the strength of this therapeutic alliance or bond is a function of the length of time a client has been in therapy. (p. 27)

In a survey of 91 adults who completed a course of solution focused brief therapy in a community mental health clinic, and who were interviewed after the final session, 89 rated the therapist as 8 or above on a 0 to 10 scale. This was with a median number of 4.5 sessions (Simon & Nelson, 2004).

de Shazer (1988) writes about the fit between the clinician and the client. There are two processes that account for a positive client/therapist alliance. First is the direction or goal of the client, the second is the mutuality.

Direction/Goal

The clinician asks questions to help the client articulate and clarify the desired direction of their work together. Without such direction, the clinical work becomes bogged down and often the client begins to perceive the work as endless and repetitive (see *Troubleshooting* later in this chapter). I have often heard clients complain about former therapies, stating that they seemed to talk endlessly about the problem and nothing ever seemed to change. It is a necessity that the client details the direction in which he or she wishes to go, and the clinician articulates to the satisfaction of the client his or her understanding of that direction. The congruence between the goal statement and the clinician's acceptance and understanding results in the client's perception that he or she and the therapist are on the same page.

Mutuality

When a clinician accepts and operates within a client's world view, the client perceives that the clinician respects him or her. This sense of respect is key to co-creating a positive clinical relationship. The clinician enhances mutuality by actively listening and responding to the client. The clinician's questions should be formulated based solely on the client's responses. The client then perceives that the clinician values and respects their world view when there is congruence in the response/question set. Conversely, mutuality suffers when the client senses that the clinician's agenda has taken priority.

Pre-Session Questions

The clinical work begins even before the client picks up the telephone to make an appointment with a clinician. The very intention of seeking help requires a presumption that the situation can and will be better. The client must have in his or her mind that meeting with a counselor will inevitably make a difference. That picture may not yet be in focus, but to a large extent, the clinician's job is to help the client clarify the difference.

When I receive an initial call from a potential client, after we have set an appointment date and time, I will say to him or her something similar to this:

> Let's suppose that our meeting together makes a difference for you – no sense doing this if it doesn't make a difference. You might not notice it immediately – it may take a day or two, or maybe even a week. But, ultimately, how will you know that our conversation will be useful?

I then inform him or her that I plan to ask them that question when we get together for our first session.

This question has potential meaning on several levels. It informs the client in what I'm interested, the direction of our conversation together, and it suggests that the context of the change will be in the client's life outside of the counseling office. Further, it tells the client that he or she is responsible for establishing a goal.

Questions About Future Change

When I first meet with clients, I will gather information about their interests, their social resources, and their jobs. I then remind them of the pre-session question and begin the process of goal setting. As they tell me about their thoughts regarding the results of their healing, I will ask for greater detail: How will they notice the difference, and how will significant others in their lives notice the difference? Throughout our conversation together, the topic of future change will be the undercurrent.

The Miracle Question

Berg and Miller (1992) write about wording the Miracle Question:

> Suppose that one night, while you are asleep, there is a miracle and the problem that brought you into therapy is solved. However, because you are asleep you don't now that the miracle has already happened. When you wake up in the morning, what will be different that will tell you that the miracle has taken place? What else? (p. 13)

The common mistake that beginning solution focused practitioners make is neglecting to contextualize the miracle question. Asking the Miracle Question without a context will often result in unrealistic responses. This is especially true in end-of-life and bereavement counseling. With adequate preparation, the clinician receive response such as, "I wouldn't be dying," or "I wou find my [deceased] husband lying next to me on the bed the rare times that I've received such a response, I have to pause to see if they might respond with a more useful answer. If not, I might say, "Well, let's suppose that it's a smaller miracle."

The following exchange, from an actual case, will serve to illustrate how the Miracle Question can be contextualized and asked. The client, Susan, is a 21-year-old female. She is an aspiring actress working as a waitress. Susan's mother died less than a month prior and Susan now complains of anxiety, inability to sleep, and "panic attacks." She has a number of family members in the area and reports having many friends.

Joel: So, I asked you a question on the phone.
Susan: Yeah.
Joel: Supposing that our talk together is helpful and you might not notice immediately – may take a day or two – how would you know?
Susan: I guess maybe a little bit of clarity. I would have clarity with my emotions and thoughts; maybe a peacefulness. I would feel because of this understanding. Because right now I have a lot of questions and there's a lot of confusion. Or maybe acceptance; I think talking to someone about it in a professional field can help me. The hardest thing for me is not to have any answers.
Joel: What will be helpful to me is to get a clearer picture.
Susan: Yeah.
Joel: So let me ask you a question that I think helps me do that. I find the clearer you are about your destination, the greater the chance of getting there.
Susan: Absolutely.
Joel: Here's a question that will help me move in that direction.

Discussion: It is usual that when initially asked about their goals for counseling, clients will present both statements of what they do not want to be happening and statements of positive goals. As in Susan's case, these initial positive goals are often stated in global terms: "greater clarity" and "understanding." I think of the global statement of positive goals as the client's initial "statement of difference." This can take many different forms: "get through the process," "get back to being my old self," or "get back into life" are some of the common ones I've heard. It is this statement of difference that is the clue for me that it is time to ask the Miracle Question.

In the above example, I begin by telling Susan that I have a question that will help me clarify her goal. This serves two purposes: 1) The Miracle Question is not necessarily meant to help her, but me. Most clients want to be helpful to the clinician and are more than willing to do so if given direction. 2) It creates a logical context for what might otherwise seem to be a strangely speculative question. The purpose of the miracle question is to help the clinician and client, together, develop a greater clarification of a useful direction.

Joel: *Let's suppose that after we talk today you're going to leave – you're going to do what you normally do. Tonight you're going to go home…*

Susan: To Manhattan.

Joel: *To Manhattan and you're going to go to sleep. Okay?* [Susan nods in agreement.] *And let's suppose that while you're sleeping, some miracle happens.*

Susan: Umm.

Joel: *And because of this miracle this clarity, this peacefulness, this acceptance, these answers happen just like that.* [I snap my fingers.] *Okay?*

Susan: Umm.

Joel: *But you can't know about it – not yet.*

Susan: I can't know about it.

Joel: *Not yet. The only way that you can know about this miracle is when you wake up tomorrow, these small changes or differences that clue you into this miracle.*

Susan: Umm.

Joel: *So that's my question. You wake up tomorrow, you open your eyes. What will be happening that would clue you into this miracle? What would be different?*

Susan: Oh, gosh, so many things could be different.

Joel: *Start somewhere.*

Susan: Maybe the heaviness would be lifted off my physical body. Physically, I've been really tense and anxious. Being able to release that. That would be one. Waking up not feeling like I'm going to throw up.

Joel: *You'd wake up and how would you be feeling instead?*

Susan: Lighter. Lighter mentally, not as many thoughts. Sometimes I'm having negative thoughts.

Joel: *So, instead of having those negative thoughts what…*

Susan: More positive thoughts.
Joel: *Like what?*
Susan: Maybe, "What a beautiful day." I'd notice that the sun is out. Seeing some light at the end of my tunnel for the day. I wouldn't be dreading going into work.
Joel: *How would you be thinking about work instead?*
Susan: Maybe I could go into work and feel a bit more positive, "This is what I'm doing just for now." Maybe I would have an epiphany and go, "I don't need to waitress anymore." I'd have this great clear idea of what I was supposed to do to substitute it and would happen. I wouldn't even have to go to work.
Joel: *What's the range of possibilities?*
Susan: I guess working with kids, working with terminally ill kids. I could get paid and have a freelance job. Maybe I could get a job teaching Yoga. Job opportunities would become clearer and I could walk away from waitressing.
Joel: *What's the smallest piece of that miracle that would be happening tomorrow after you wake up?*
Susan: I guess my friend would call me about taking Yoga and she would say, "Come in today; we're going to do some sessions. We're going to release your body and I'm going to teach you about Yoga."
Joel: *How do you think that would make a difference for you?*
Susan: It would give me a chance to release a little bit. I feel that my mind is more sometime released than my body.
Joel: *So, when your mind is released a little bit more, what's happening? How do you know that?*
Susan: I'm not as emotional. I'm calmer, centered, grounded.
Joel: *Okay, how do you know that?*
Susan: I'm not throwing myself on the floor and crying. [She laughs.]
Joel: *What are you doing instead?*
Susan: There's a glimmer of hope behind my thoughts, "I'm going to be okay." Intuitively, I have a sense that I'm a little more at peace.

Discussion: Often there is confusion of the intention of the Miracle Question. When I ask the question, I do not expect that something miraculous will happen to the client. As was discussed in Chapter 4, the solution-building language-game is different from the problem-solving language-game. As the approach developed, the thrust was away from problem to solution talk. The Miracle Question evolved for two main reasons: 1) to invite the client into an alternative language-game whereby knowing more about the problem is no longer essential to the clinical process, and 2) to help bring the client's goal into sharper focus (de Shazer, 1991). The effect of the Miracle Question is, essentially, to guide the conversation away from greater details of problems to greater details of possible solutions.

In asking the Miracle Question, I have found it useful to include several minor, but effective, variations. Instead of asking about the problem, I incorporated Susan's statement of difference – "clarity, peacefulness and acceptance." Since for the bereaved client, the "problem" is the death of a significant other, the logical response to eliminating the problem is that the loved one would still be alive. Using the client's statement of change increases the probability that the described miracle will be both practical and possible.

The other addition is the use of the word "yet." Very often clients will initially respond by wanting to know how the miracle happened. When asking the question in the past, I have often heard the client ask something similar to, "Does this miracle happen in a dream?" When I started to include the word "yet," it appeared to obviate the need for clients to understand the agency of the miracle. Clients are more amenable to suspending belief and accepting that the miracle happens without needing to know how or why.

In asking Susan the Miracle Question, I was careful to pace her to ensure that she was making useful meaning of the question. The concept "yes-set" might be useful here, as well. The yes-set was first described Dr. Milton Erickson (Hammond, 1990). The yes-set is created when the clinician asks a series of questions to which the client would likely answer in the affirmative. Once the yes-set is established, the clinician can then ask a question where the response is less predictable. The creation of the yes-set makes it more probable that the client will answer the more doubtful question in the affirmative.

The Miracle Question is a good example of how the yes-set operates. In the example, I begin by describing that the client and I will be having a conversation, she leaves and has her normal day, then goes home and, finally, goes to sleep. Susan clearly acknowledges the pace; there are several times she indicates by nodding her head and verbally responds. She even adds to the statement that she goes home – "to Manhattan." Essentially, I am creating a pattern of positive responses that will serve to increase the probability that she will accept the improbable – a miracle will happen. The miracle is wrapped into the normal events of the client's life and the improbable miracle becomes probable because it is transformed into a logical extension of the normal events in the Susan's ordinary day.

It is evident that the Miracle Question provides a useful context for Susan. She responds, "Oh gosh, so many things would be different." Essentially, she has been invited and accepts the invitation into a solution-building conversation. This does not mean that her responses will always be consistent with solution building. Clients usually alternate between solution and problem talk. Their responses are often vague and global.

Beyond separating the solution from the problem, the miracle question has two additional positive effects: 1) it provides an anchor for solution talk, and 2) it allows for greater detail of the solution picture. Citing Miller and de Shazer, Simon and Nelson (2007) reference the concept of anchor:

> Gale Miller observed that devices such as the miracle question or scaling could be used as session anchors. When the conversation moves in a potentially less-than-useful direction, the therapist can always return to the miracle question to re-anchor the conversation toward solution talk. (p. 65)

As is often the case, the client will return to describing the problem. The clinician need only reference the Miracle Question in order to bring the conversation back on track. The following dialogue from the session with Susan is an example:

Joel: *You said one of the things that would be happening would be acceptance.*
Susan: Accepting where I am. That's the hardest thing.
Joel: *Okay. You wake up tomorrow and this miracle happens and at least you're starting that direction. How would you know? How would you be thinking differently? What would you be doing?*
Susan: I guess I would be less critical of myself. I would be not be dreading my work, not very depressed. I would want to go outside; I would want to sit in the sun. I would want to exercise. I wouldn't feel so heavy. I would just be present. Because all this other stuff gets involved.
Joel: *You said "less critical."*
Susan: Of where I am right now.
Joel: *Of where you are right now. How would your thinking change?*

Susan: Maybe I would be able to quit my job and not worry about finances. I don't think I'm ever going to feel better until I'm out of waitressing.

Later on in the session, Susan and I together provide another example of re-anchoring the miracle question:

Joel: *You said that there's a relationship between this glimmer of hope and facing the death of your mom.*

Susan: Yeah.

Joel: *What's the relationship?*

Susan: Well that...I don't even really know. The glimmer of hope is that it's going to bring me to some real understanding...I have to ask myself, "Why did this have to happen now?" I'm on the brink of womanhood. It was a sudden death. "So," I say to myself, "What could this possibly mean, what can I learn from this?" That sort of thing.

Joel: *And your answer to that question?*

Susan: Oh, I don't have an answer.

Joel: *Let's say that the miracle happens and you did have an answer. What did you learn from this?*

Susan: I guess the only thing that would come out of this, that would make sense, is that it would propel me to the path my spirit was meant to go on. For the past year, I've been feeling very unbalanced. I guess this would bring a greater spiritual awakening and it would propel me in the right direction. I hate to say, "I feel a bit lost," but I do.

Joel: *So you wake up from this miracle and the smallest thing that would tell you were starting to move in the right direction. What would that be? How would you be thinking differently? What would you be doing?*

Susan: I guess I would be less critical of myself; I would not be dreading my work; not very depressed. I would want to go outside, I would want to sit in the sun, I would want to exercise.

Discussion: After I asked Susan what meaning she would take from her mother's death and how it would be helpful, she responds that she does not know. I quickly re-anchor the Miracle Question, and this appears to have given her a useful framework in which to think about and answer that question. The rest of the discussion centers on co-constructing the details of that miracle picture.

In my experience, initially clients often view the miracle through the veil of the abstract. Susan states that the miracle would result in her having "acceptance," a physical release, and making meaning of death.

It then becomes the clinician's job to help the client transform these vague and, as of yet, meaningless phrases into a more detailed and concrete picture. The clearer the direction for the client, the greater chance that he or she will leave the conversation and do something that will be both different and more helpful. The end result of that conversation is a clearer picture: Susan would go outside, sit in the sun, and exercise.

The additional advantage of the Miracle Question is that it paradoxically results in greater details of the solution picture. As Susan co-constructs the details of the miracle, it becomes evident that her solution is less global and somewhat more practical: she finds her current waitress job unrewarding. This does not mean that the solution will be easy, since she still needs to make money to pay her rent, etc. Recall that one of the assumptions of solution focus is that the client has the personal and social resources. As Susan becomes clearer about what will be most helpful to her, I needed to keep that assumption in mind and think that there is a good chance that she will do something to move in the right direction. There is no predicting what that might be; clients are creative, wise, and have the capacity to figure things out once the road map becomes clearer. My job is to help both of us make useful meaning of the difference and this, in turn, will move her toward even more changes.

The number of times I asked Susan to elucidate how her thinking will be changing after the miracle is of special note. There is a paradoxical element to this question and response: Susan can only answer that question by actually thinking differently.

Exception Questions

Exceptions are times when the problem is not happening, happening less, or is not the client's central focus. When I first began practicing solution focus, it was typical to ask clients about exceptions to the problem early in the session before asking the miracle question. What I found is that while clients reported exceptions, the exceptions did not seem to be significant enough to help deconstruct the problem. It was only when exceptions arose after the Miracle Question that they seemed to have significance for the client. I have found most often that because the exceptions arose spontaneously, it is not even necessary to separately ask about them. Here is an example of a spontaneous exception in Susan's case:

Susan: Two days ago I couldn't even get out of bed. Two days later I was okay. I was feeling very grounded and having very positive thoughts.

Joel: So when were you having...
Susan: Two days ago.
Joel: Grounded and having...
Susan: Yeah, I was saying, "Okay, you can't do this to yourself. Your mother wouldn't want you to do this. She's still with you. She's not gone."
Joel: That thought was helpful?
Susan: Yeah, it was [as if] I was giving myself a pep talk.

Discussion: It is often useful to ask about exceptions in the context of the day after the miracle happens. Here is another example of this:

Joel: What pieces of this miracle have happened already?
Susan: I've come to talk to somebody – that's the first step.
Joel: Okay.
Susan: Seeking out spiritual seminars and reading. Those are the three things. Seeking out someone to speak to and being a little more vocal about it.

Discussion: It is then possible to expand on each of these elements and have Susan describe how they happen and what difference each element makes for her.

Scaling Questions

In the following vignette, I use scaling with Susan:

Joel: Let's do this. If I had a scale of zero to ten.
Susan: Mmm.
Joel: Ten is the miracle. Zero is maybe a couple of weeks ago. Where would you put yourself?
Susan: I have to say, like, three.
Joel: Three's not bad. How come?
Susan: I think half-way there would be semi... maybe three is that you're about to realize it. Five would be accepting it. The rest would be moving through whatever accepting brings.
Joel: You said that three is about to realize it. What tells you that?
Susan: I'm getting more waves of the realization. Or more thoughts of, "Wow, this is really happening." I'm working toward the steps of trying to heal. Whatever that is. I find myself doing more of

that – working towards that. So, I go, "This is my life now," to really see it. The thoughts are more present.

Joel: *What else puts you at three?*

Susan: I've definitely come a little ways because three weeks ago, I was feeling like there was a numbness that was coming over me. So you're numb, and unsure, and unclear of really what's happening. As you move, things are a little more clear. I'm starting to realize that I'm going to do that spiritual seminar. I'm clear about what I want to do. I've never felt that way before. Yoga – that's clear it's something I need to do. Just moving in that direction. Also, I'm able to sleep a little bit more.

Joel: *If your cousin were here and I asked her that same scale, where do you think she'd put you?*

Susan: I think maybe the same.

Joel: *About a three?*

Susan: About a three or a four, yeah. Because we talk a lot.

Joel: *What is she hearing from you that tells you that she would put you at three or four?*

Susan: I know she's seen me in bad shape. She's also seen me and I'm going, "I'm having a good day today." I don't feel really too emotional about things. I can think about it and be clearer. She said I should go to the gym and I would feel better. I told her I don't feel like it, but I ended up going to the gym one day.

Joel: *Even though you didn't want to?*

Susan: Yeah.

Joel: *How did you do that?*

Susan: "Once I get off the treadmill, I'll feel better."

Joel: *That's what you were thinking?*

Susan: Yeah.

Joel: *And was that true?*

Susan: I feel better after I exercise.

Joel: *If Mom were around, where would she put you on that scale?*

Susan: Maybe Mom would say that I'm further along than I think.

Joel: *Oh, how come?*

Susan: I'm where I need to be and the questions I'm asking myself are all the right questions. It's very painful, but I'm right where I should be. If my mother were watching, she would say that I'm right where I need to be. "You don't know it, cause it's not supposed to be revealed to you yet, and you're further along than you think."

Joel: *If things went from three to four, how would you know?*

Susan: I guess I would have less negative thought[s], I would be able to tolerate work, and I wouldn't be devastated by the break-up with my boyfriend.

Joel: *So, what would be going on instead that would move you just one point?*

Susan: I'd feel strong inside, that I could do this on my own. I wouldn't have as many open-ended questions.

Joel: *I think we're at eight on the scale right now.*

Susan: What do you mean?

Joel: *That would kind of put you at eight on the scale.*

Susan: Oh, okay, okay.

Joel: *How would you know that you're at four?*

Susan: I'd want to get up tomorrow and work out, and feel good, and feel alive.

Joel: *You'd get up and go to the gym?*

Susan: Yeah.

Joel: *That you'd want to, or that you would do it?*

Susan: That I would get up, want to, and then do it.

Joel: *I want to ask one more scale that will help me with my thinking, and then take that break. On a scale of zero to ten and ten is pretty much anything I might suggest – as long as it were legal, no one got hurt, and it didn't cost you anything – you'd do anything, any crazy idea I might come up with.*

Susan: I'd try it.

Joel: *Where would you be on that scale?*

Susan: Like a ten! I'd do it!

Joel: *You just gave me a blank check, you know that don't you?* [Both laugh.]

It is usual for clinicians first experimenting with scaling to view numbers in concrete terms and to express disappointment when clients place themselves relatively lower on a scale. In response to a scale where ten represents the miracle, Susan responds three. There are several ways of misunderstanding three: (1) three is lower than four through ten; (2) three is higher than zero, one, and two; (3) exceptions to the problem are inherent within any number above zero; (4) since ten has been defined as the miracle Susan described, three represents that some pieces of the miracle must already be occurring.

In fact, no matter how high or how low clients place themselves on the scale, as long as they state any number above zero, the preceding misunderstandings are possible. The experienced solution focused practitioner merely views scaling as another opportunity to co-construct meanings with the client (Berg & de Shazer, 1993).

The major consideration for the clinician is which dialogue will most likely engage the client in a useful conversation. After Susan responds that she is at a three on the Miracle Scale, I state, "That's not bad, how come?" This is a clear indication that my interest is in viewing three as higher than zero, rather than lower than ten. It is clear from her response that she accepts my meaning and is willing to engage in a conversation of how three differs from zero. Had she responded differently, I could still invite her into a solution-building conversation using scaling.

For example, she might have responded, "I'm having trouble accepting the death of my mother." This would have been a clear indication that she was making meaning of three as less than ten. Based upon similar situations, I most likely would have responded, "Of course, that certainly explains why you're not at a ten. I wonder how come you're not lower than three?" Or, "How is three different than zero, one, or two?"

Continuing the conversation with Susan, I sought greater details of the exceptions of three. She responds that at three she is becoming more accepting of her mother's death, having begun to move beyond a sense of numbness. In my experience, many clients respond that their initial reaction to a significant other's death is a sense of disbelief and numbness. They then relate that once they come to the realization that the other is no longer living, they experience a tremendous amount of sadness. My choices are to have a discussion with Susan around that profound sadness or how acceptance might be useful despite the pain that it might bring.

Susan responds that acceptance has brought a greater clarity about what might constitute a useful direction for her. My next question is how Susan might view her progress through someone else's eyes – her cousin. This serves to continue the solution-building conversation, expand on details of the exceptions, and assist Susan to describe behaviors, rather than focus on feelings.

Susan responds that her cousin would also put her at three because the cousin knows about days where Susan is less emotional and clearer. This is another example of Wittgenstein's statement "inner process stands in need of outward criteria." Asking Susan to view herself through someone else's eyes requires her to describe behavior rather than report inner states.

Next, I ask Susan where her mother would put her on that scale. I have found that this is a way of using the deceased significant other as part of a conversation around healing. Susan's response is very typical; from her point of view, her mother knows that while this is a painful process, Susan is "right where I need to be," and maybe even further than she thinks. This latter statement is paradoxical. As soon as Susan states that (from her mother's view) she is "further along than you think," Susan accepts the statement as being real and this allows her to search for signs that she is, indeed, further along.

The next part of scaling is addressing future exceptions. I ask Susan how she would know that things went from three to four. Other practitioners may prefer to ask what the client might do to move up the scale. My preference is to have the client describe how things would be just a bit better rather than suggest agency of change. There are many ways in which four could happen. Some of those are because of the client's actions, others may occur because of some other individual, or some may just happen because of chance occurrences. There is a greater possibility of a difference happening when the question invites the client to describe the change rather than how the change might happen.

As is often the case, Susan describes a change that would most likely be greater than just one step higher on the scale, and very often the difference is described in vague terms. For example, Susan responds that four would be "I'd feel strong inside, that I could do this on my own, I wouldn't have as many open-ended questions."

In response, I ask Susan to consider something much smaller and more concrete. She simply answers that she would get up and work out. We have already discussed how exercise has been useful for her and has been a helpful exception to her feelings of grief. Challenging the client to think about the details rather than the global statements of change is also a way of assuring that the clinician is following the sage advice, "Always go more slowly than the client."

Although I chose to use a miracle scale in this case, I had other choices as well. I could have scaled Susan on acceptance, clarity, or a sense of balance. These were all words that Susan had used during the conversation. Each one would have probably taken a different, but equally useful, direction. In general, the most useful scales are based on the clients' descriptions of difference, as these help to further engage them.

It is also possible to use several different scales during the course of a session. I asked Susan to scale her willingness to take a suggestion. I have often used this scale and have found it useful in considering what suggestion I might offer and the client's level of customership. I could have scaled Susan on her confidence that she will reach four as she described previously, or asked Susan what the first signs of four might be even before four actually happened. The types of scales are limitless and each serves to simply co-construct prior, current, and future exceptions.

Coping Questions

The initial job of the clinician is to invite the client into a solution-building conversation. Depending on the client, this may take a great deal of patience and gentle questioning. Many clients are experiencing much pain and sense of loss. It should always be remembered that this is solution focused – not solution *forced* – practice. There are rare times that clients' perception of pain initially precludes them from considering a more useful direction. For them, the sense of loss is constant and they may have difficulty envisioning a different and better future.

When the conversation with the client takes this tack, it is much too easy for the clinician to become frustrated, impatient, and to characterize the client as being resistant. A much more useful frame is to not only have a sense of what the client might be experiencing, but also to see beyond the pain to the strength that is required for the client to endure. In these situations, it is often helpful to ask coping questions. I have often stated something similar to: "This has been a difficult time for you. What is it that keeps you going day after day? How did you just get up out of bed and come here to see me?"

This usually invites clients to move in several possibly useful directions: talk about their inner strength, and/or talk about the hope that the conversation with me might make some difference. Either answer allows the clinician to expand on the response and to engage the client in solution building.

Taking the Break

In the beginning of the first session, I inform the client that I will take a short break sometime during the session to think about their situation and will return to share my thoughts with them. I have taught solution focus for a good portion of the past 16 years. I have known many professionals who have decided to practice solution focus. To my amazement, many of them have felt uncomfortable about and have decided not to practice the break. When I have asked about their decision, there have been a variety of answers: "I don't have the space," "I don't have the time," "I can't leave the client unsupervised," and "I just don't feel comfortable." I have found, wherever I have practiced, that I could take the opportunity to take a session break even if it meant having the client sit in my office while I sat at my desk, and wrote down some ideas to share.

The fact is that even though taking a break may be something new for the clinician, the client assumes that this is just part of the clinician's practice and something he or she has done in the past. Explaining that the break is useful to the clinician in helping to organize his or her thoughts is sufficient explanation for most clients. I cannot recall one client who has ever complained that I took a session break. Conversely, I have had many clients who have responded that this is a good idea and thanked me for taking the time to think about them.

During the break, I have found it useful to include a template that includes several elements: normalizing, restructuring (including a solvable problem), affirmation of competencies, bridging statement, and suggestions (Campbell et al., 1999). Susan's case may help to illustrate each of these points.

Joel: *First, thank you giving me the chance to work with you.*
Susan: Thank you, maybe I should take notes.
Joel: *Well, we'll see if I say anything of use to you [both laugh]. The only guarantee is that I'll do my best. I assume that you will, too, and we'll see what happens. The first thing – obvious – is we're only talking about a month – not even a month [since your mother's death].*
Susan: Yeah.
Joel: *So, it's pretty early. I agree that you're probably where you need to be right now. One thing I've learned from doing this is that there's a large range of what's normal. People do what they need to do and they do it in their own time and own way. The question is whether what you're doing is making a difference. I think that you've been doing some useful thinking – we'll see, but I think you have been. And you're right, part of that may be painful, but also part of that might be uplifting.*
Susan: Yeah.
Joel: *I think, in this culture, we get stuck in either/or thinking – either it's painful or it's uplifting. When, in fact, it can be both at the same time.*
Susan: Yeah, I'm going through a lot of that.
Joel: *And I think sometimes we get so tuned into one that we don't see the other. Sometimes I think that's part of my job; tap people on the*

shoulder and say, "you're looking here and you ought to be looking there."

Susan: Yeah.

Joel: *In some ways, I think you're ahead of where I would expect you to be. I think Mom's right. You've found some things that have been useful to you: exercising, doing some useful thinking that helps you see some light at the end of the tunnel – not clear yet but it's getting there. Yeah, so I think in some ways you're a little further than I would expect.*

Susan: Oh, good!

Joel: *Right, and I would assume that no matter what you're experiencing, it's normal, because it probably is. I've also learned working here that healing is an active process. It's not a noun, it's a verb. I think an example is going to the gym when you don't want to. And knowing that once you get off the machine, you're going to feel better. I know that getting there…*

Susan: Is the hard part.

Joel: *Is the hard part. But once you're there, you're there. Part of the healing is doing the hard part. You asked me to think about the "anxiety and fear." I think that goes around with that either/or, both/ and idea. There are going to be times that you experience that and there are other times that you're going to be experiencing something very different. You told me that. There are times that you feel more peaceful and more spiritual. It's a question of where you focus.*

Susan: Okay, that's a good way of looking at it.

Joel: *I do have a suggestion. I thought maybe I'd use your acting skills. This is not the answer. Basically, this would give me more information – it's something to learn from. Each evening before you go to bed for the next week, you're going to flip a coin [I flip a coin as I am saying this]. If the coin comes up heads, you're going to go to sleep and you're going to act as much as possible as if the next day is your Miracle Day. Even if it's an hour. If half a day, terrific; if the whole day, great. If it comes up tails, have your regular day. I want you to notice the difference. It's an experiment – we'll see what happens.*

Susan: Absolutely, I'll definitely try it.

There are a number of normalizing statements: the time frame is relatively short, how most people react is normal, and everyone has their own way and time frame. I suggest some restructuring possibilities as well: it is both/and not either/or, it is a question of where she decides to focus (to which she states "that's a good way of looking at it"), the healing process is inherent within the "hard part," and healing is an active process. Clients often come to see a clinician because they believe that their problems are complicated and unsolvable. It is useful to help clients restructure their thinking about the problem, itself, so that the original problem is deconstructed and then a more solvable problem can be co-constructed.

I compliment her for being ahead of where I would expect her to be, for the good thinking that she has already been doing, for having times of feeling peaceful and more spiritual, and going to the gym even when she does not feeling like it, since she will know that it will make her feel better.

I am about to give her a suggestion and want to put it in a context of what I have just explained to her. This raises the probability that she will see the connection between the main body of the break message and the suggestion and, therefore, is more amenable to trying the suggestion. This is called the "bridging statement" and, in this example, I explain to Susan that this is a learning experience that will give us more useful information, an experiment, and will utilize her acting abilities.

In designing a break, I attempt to take into account the reason Susan was a customer (see Chapter 4). Since she had scaled at ten on the effort scale, I decided to try a more active suggestion. The level of customership is one consideration that needs to be taken into account when designing a suggestion. Other considerations are the open-ended nature of the suggestion; suggestions that essentially build upon past, present, and future exceptions.

My tendency is to enhance possibilities inherent within any suggestion. I could have suggested that Susan attend the gym for a specific number of days during the week. This would have narrowly focused her on only one useful activity rather than suggest that she notice other things along with exercise that will be helpful to her. These may include actions that she will take or random life events – specifically those that are useful to her. How the positive changes have taken place is of far less importance than making the changes real through co-constructive conversations.

I have also learned that the probability that the client will follow the suggestion decreases when the suggestion is too specific. This makes sense, since specific suggestions may not be congruent within the client's own life context. In general, the best suggestions are ones in which the client is already engaged, and the client states have been useful.

Suggestions are useful when they focus the client on exceptions. The Miracle Day suggestion will hopefully serve to focus Susan on the present, and how her life continues to improve while the problem becomes less problematic. I could have asked Susan to notice what moves her one point on the scale, or to guess what others might be noticing different about her. The possibilities are virtually limitless, but suggestions should always take into account customership.

If the client opts to return, it is not my usual practice to ask clients whether or not they have tried the suggestion. By definition, suggestions refer only to considerations of future action. My assumption is that if clients choose not to do as I've suggested, he or she will find an alternative that will be more congruent within his or her contexts. If the client returns, my job then is to find out how the client has moved in a positive direction.

There is a story that was told by Milton Erickson (Gordon & Meyer-Anderson, 1981; Rosen, 1982), that one day he was returning from high school and noticed a horse that had wandered away from his owner. Erickson jumped on the horse, led it to the road, and then let the horse choose the direction. Once in a while, the horse attempted to graze on the side of the road and Erickson pulled on the reins to keep the horse moving.

After a while, the horse turned down a farm road and, as it approached the house, the farmer came out. He looked at Erickson, looked at the horse, and commented that this was certainly his horse, but he never had seen the rider before. He marveled that Erickson would know where the horse belongs. Erickson responded that he didn't; the horse knew where he lives. Erickson just kept him on the road. Chapter 9 discusses how to use subsequent visits to metaphorically "keep the client on the road."

TROUBLESHOOTING: COMMON ISSUES IN SOLUTION FOCUSED PRACTICE

It is usual for those first learning solution focus to struggle with maintaining a solution-building conversation. Most clinicians were trained in problem solving methodologies and the transition is often a difficult one, but one worth pursuing. At times, the clinician can feel that he or she is going in circles and little is being accomplished. There are several reasons why this might happen.

Who Is the Customer?

It is important to know who is the customer for change. It is a mistake to assume and act as if the person in front of the clinician is the one who wants something to be different. People come to see a counselor for many reasons: they want something to be different, they want someone else to change, someone else wants them to change, and/or someone has mandated that they see a counselor. Sessions seem to be on an endless loop when the clinician acts as if the individual is a customer for change, when in fact he or she is not. Right from the onset, it behooves the counselor to ask clients who it is that wants them to be there, and what are the hoped-for differences that the client and/or the other person wants. This can be simply done by asking clients in initial phone calls to think about how the conversation might make a difference for them and then to begin there at the first session.

What Is the Client a Customer for?

When a clinician asks a client what he or she wants to be different, it is usual for the client to respond in the negative: "I don't want to cry all the time," "I don't want to be sitting around and grieving," or "I don't want to be sad." Counseling is facilitated when clients can describe the details of the difference in positive terms, from their own points-of-view, and the points-of-view of others in their lives.

Is the Goal Clear?

Especially in bereavement and end-of-life counseling, goals are often expressed in vague terms: "I want to get on with life," "I want to get through the process," or "I want to be me again." The clinician needs to transform the vague into the concrete by helping the client describe the goal statement in observable behavioral terms. Solution-focused questions, and especially the Miracle Question, are ideal for this purpose.

Is the Goal Realistic?

It is not enough for the goal to be described in observable terms. The goal needs to be realistic in the client's life context. The goal of having the deceased husband lying in bed alive next to the bereaved spouse is certainly concrete and observable – unfortunately, it is not realistic.

It is the client's responsibility to convince the clinician that the goal is possible.

Is the Counselor Pacing the Client?

Another reason why the counseling process seems to get stuck is that the counselor is moving too fast for the client. Only with practice, and by developing a trained ear, will the counselor learn how to pace the client and (more importantly) recognize when the counselor is moving too fast. This is often evident when the counselor and client reach an impasse together. While the tendency is to theorize this as client resistance, it is more useful to recognize it as a mismatched pace. The clinician can then slow down and let the client dictate the rate of progress.

Has the Counselor Become the Customer?

There are times that the counselor wants things to be better more for his or her sake than the client's. This is especially true with mandated clients. We all want to be successful in what we do and to be recognized as competent. When the desire to be seen as competent and successful is the overriding motivation, the clinician loses his or her objectivity, ability to listen, and respond to the client.

EVALUATING OUTCOMES: THE POST-DISCHARGE SURVEY

In December 2007, two interns involved in masters programs were placed with Hospice of Orange and Sullivan Counties. One of their assignments was to phone 35 clients who had been seen in bereavement counseling. The clients had all been seen at least six months prior to the contact. Of the 35, 26 were actually reached. One of the 26 surveyed was eliminated from the final tally. It was clear from the response that the individual was referring not to bereavement sessions, but to their experiences with Hospice prior to the death of their significant other. An additional 16 former bereavement clients were contacted later by a hospice volunteer.

All sessions followed a solution focused format as defined by the use of pre-session change questions; future oriented questions, the Miracle Question, scaling questions, a session break with or without an observing team followed by compliments, and an in-between-session suggestion. Of the 35 total, the average number of sessions was 2.6, the median was 2. Table 5.1 references the number of total sessions per client:

Table 5.1

Total No. of Sessions	1	2	3	4	7	8
No. of Clients	25	18	3	3	1	1

N = 51

Following are the questions used during the survey:

- *Question 1*: "Place yourself on the following scale in terms of your goal for bereavement counseling: 1 = no change, 2 = minimal change, 3 = moderate change, 4 = significant change, 5 = full achievement of goals."
- *Question 2*: "What part of the counseling sessions was most helpful to you?"
- *Question 3*: "Was there anything in the sessions that surprised you?"
- *Question 4*: "Is there anything we could have done differently?"
- *Question 5*: "If someone you know wanted bereavement counseling, would you feel comfortable in recommending that they contact Hospice?"
- *Question 6*: "Anything else that you would like to add?"

Question 1: "Place yourself on the following scale in terms of your goal for bereavement counseling: 1 = no change, 2 = minimal change, 3 = moderate change, 4 = significant change, 5 = full achievement of goals."

Table 5.2 represents the responses:

Table 5.2

NO CHANGE	MINIMAL CHANGE	MODERATE CHANGE	SIGNIFICANT CHANGE	FULL ACHIEVEMENT
0	4	13	7	0

Discussion: in general, meta-analysis of psychotherapy as early as 1952 suggests that approximately 67 percent of those engaged in counseling report improvement. This was later reinforced by additional outcome research. In the *Handbook of Psychotherapy and Behavior Change,* Lambert (1986) reports that 66 percent of psychotherapy clients demonstrated improvement.

While the outcome data on grief counseling is sparse, Larson and Hoyt (2007) state:

> Another approach to de-emphasizing the importance of Allumbaugh and Hoyt's (1999) findings has been distortion or misrepresentation of their conclusions. For example, Bonanno (2004) began his summary of grief intervention research by citing "two recent meta-analyses [that] independently reached the conclusion that grief-specific therapies tend to be relatively inefficacious (Kato & Mann, 1999; Neimeyer, 2000)" (pp. 21–22), then stated that "a third meta-analytic study" (Allumbaugh & Hoyt, 1999) concluded that "grief therapies can be effective but generally to a lesser degree than...other forms of psychotherapy" (p. 22). Compare this with Allumbaugh and Hoyt's own summary of their findings, cited in full above, stating that this moderate aggregate effect size reflects unrepresentative sampling procedures associated with most of these studies, and that more ecologically valid studies tend to find that grief interventions are "as effective [as] or possibly even more effective than psychotherapy in general" (p. 78). (p. 352)

Given the above, and using conventional approaches, we should expect an improvement rate equal to at least 67 percent. In this survey, 83 percent of 24 clients[1] contacted reported moderate to significant positive changes. What further impresses is that this was accomplished with a median of two sessions. The 83 percent improvement rate is consistent with outcome studies completed at BFTC (De Jong & Hopwood, 1996).

Given the ongoing nature of bereavement, it stands to reason that none of the interviewees reported full achievement of their goals for counseling. In many ways, this is a test of validity of the question.

Question 2: "What part of the counseling sessions was most helpful to you?"

Responses: 16 of 29 responded. The other responses were either blank, or "I don't remember." The following are the verbatim responses:

1. Just talking.
2. I met with a gentleman and he was very nice. He reassured me that I was doing a great job. He wanted me to come back, but I was OK. I didn't think I needed more.

---
[1] Five clients reported difficulty understanding the question.

3. Well, I guess just talking helped him understand me. He seemed like he knew what I was talking about.
4. He just listened.
5. I let my feelings out.
6. Thoughts of the future.
7. I guess just talking about it.
8. Talking about the situation and things that were upsetting me.
9. Thinking about the future and not being sad.
10. I guess talking.
11. Getting past the sadness.
12. Letting out feelings and talking.
13. I could talk about it.
14. I was told I was better off than most at this point, and was told my reaction is normal.
15. Being able to express feelings to a stranger. I felt safe to express my emotions.
16. Talking it out, and hearing all was normal.

Discussion: Given the nature of the approach, one would expect responses 2, 6, 9, and 11. In accord with solution focused practice, one would not expect the responses exemplified by 5, 7, 8, 12, 13, 15, and 16. I had similar results in a survey completed in a community mental health clinic. In a co-authored article (Simon & Nelson, 2002), I attempted to explain the disparity:

> Clients and solution focused therapists clearly spent little time in problem talk. This raises the question of why 28 percent of clients stated that problem talk was helpful? One answer has been suggested that clients do not find it necessary to engage in long-term problem talk in order to receive benefits from therapy. Perhaps if clients feel the need to tell their problem stories, they may not need to spend as much time as is commonly assumed.
> As a second possibility, it can be reasoned that clients see therapists with the hope and expectation that therapy will result in useful change. If they have been in therapy before, former therapists more than likely will have engaged them in a problem-solving process. Even if they have not had previous therapy, the popular media and culture regarding the therapeutic process may have influenced them. Finally, many clients come to therapy having discussed the process with friends and/or family who have previously been in therapy. Clients may engage in therapy with the assumptions that 1) Talking about problems will make things better. 2) Their

problem situation has improved. 3) Therefore, problem talk must have occurred. (p. 40)

de Shazer (personal communication) had an alternate explanation. He suggested that problem talk is inherent in solution-building conversations. Even without specifically referencing problems, they are still part of the conversation. Therefore, when clients talk about solutions to the issues that bring them to bereavement counselors, they are at the same time and in their own minds referencing the problem, even though they may not actually talk about the problems, per se (see Chapter 3).

Response number two is very interesting. It is not my habit to urge people to return to or leave counseling. Clients take responsibility for deciding whether further sessions will be helpful. Given the nature of brief counseling, it is not unusual for clients to state that I urged them to leave counseling; it is very unusual to hear a client state that I urged them to return.

Question 3: "Was there anything in the sessions that surprised you?"

Six clients responded:

1. That I can be happy again.
2. That I could look at the future optimistically.
3. Thinking of suicide and talking about it to someone else.
4. That [the counselor] cared. That he showed compassion.
5. I was left alone to think.
6. I was surprised to hear that others had seen angels too.

Discussion: The first two seem to be congruent to the solution focused approach. The fourth one is a bit surprising: I'm not sure why it would surprise this person that someone in the business of providing bereavement counseling should care and show compassion.

Question 4: "Is there anything we could have done differently?"

There were four responses to this question:

1. Come more times.
2. Went more times, I guess.

3. Come more times; one time didn't help.
4. The room was changed from one to another. The room was cold and impersonal and there were outside interferences.

Discussion: Even though 96 percent of clients came 4 sessions or less, only 3 of 29 (10 percent) voiced wanting more sessions. As previously stated, it is my practice to remain neutral regarding the question of further sessions. It might be useful for me in the future to emphasize to clients that the decision for further sessions is the province of the client. It should be further noted that none of the three sought additional services either from Hospice or another professional.

Reviewing Table 5.1, it should be noted that 25 of 51 (49 percent) of clients in this survey attended only one session. This number, combined with those that attended two sessions, account for 84 percent of the 51 total clients. The average number of sessions was 1.9. De Jong and Hopwood (op. cit.) reported that at BFTC, 80 percent of 275 cases came for 4 or fewer sessions. The average number of sessions was 2.9.

In my experience, most clients coming for bereavement counseling assume that healing is probable, and that treatment will be brief. This may account for the fact that those engaged in solution focused bereavement averaged fewer sessions than in mental health services.

More traditional theories of counseling would characterize those that did not return after only one session as treatment failures. Outcome data suggest that a single session is the modal number of sessions for all therapies, independent of the clinician's orientation. Contrary to characterizing one-session contracts as failures, most clients expressed that the one session was helpful and sufficient (Miller, et al., 1997).

Question 5: "If someone you know wanted bereavement counseling, would you feel comfortable in recommending that they contact Hospice?"

Of the 29 who responded to this question, 25 (86 percent) stated that they would recommend Hospice bereavement services. Two stated that they were not sure. One of the two had rated their change as moderate. The other is the person who stated, "Come more times; one time didn't help." There were only two people who answered in the negative. One of the two stated that he or she did not remember having the session.

Discussion: 86 percent of the 29 were clear that they would recommend Hospice bereavement. Two were unsure and one stated they would not, based on the rationale that they did not recall attending a bereavement session.

An Appropriate Anecdote: I saw a woman for three sessions. Each time she placed herself at zero on the scale and reported little progress. She talked about outside interests that she had been active in pursuing prior to the death of her husband, and her Miracle Day included these activities as being healing for her. In the span of two months since I first saw her, she had not made any attempt to engage in healing activities as she had defined them.

After taking a break during the third session, I returned and explained that, obviously, our work together was not making a difference. I wondered whether at this time progress was even possible and, perhaps, she might need to be where she is for some time. I suggested that we take a break and that when she noticed that she was higher on the scale, she should give me a call and we can discuss what is different. The woman was very wise and responded, "So, what you're telling me is that it's up to me to get moving."

While I do not believe that she was very happy with my suggestion, she called me several months later to tell me that she had indeed become involved in a quilting club, was now walking every day, and was feeling much better. She was quick to add that our sessions together had not really been very helpful to her at all. The moral may be that solution focus is not a therapy to be practiced by therapists who need to have clients tell them that the therapist is the reason that the client healed.

Question 6: "Anything else that you would like to add?"

There were five responses:

1. Coming one time was not enough to get over losing my husband.
2. It's nice to have this service in the community.
3. The sessions were great and very helpful.
4. Thank you, Joel.
5. As a man, I thought counseling would be hard to do, but found it to be good.

PROVISO

It is clear that this is not meant to be a "scientific study" and that the results, obviously, do not represent rigorous research. Rather, it is an attempt to learn from clients directly whether they perceived that bereavement sessions using a solution focused brief approach was helpful to them, and perhaps which elements they found helpful. The thought here is that if others are willing to engage in similar studies, we might begin to accumulate enough information that will point in useful directions. A major stance of solution focus is creating a therapy inductively by listening to clients telling us what works.

Applying Solution Focused Brief Practice to End-of-Life and Grief Counseling

PART III

6 Stories of Healing: Solution Focus and the Dying Patient

> All that lives must die, Passing through nature to eternity.
> —*William Shakespeare,*
> **Hamlet,** *Act I, Scene 2*

When we talk about the meaning of healing, it is usually associated with the physical. Hospice works with those for whom physical healing is no longer a viable option. Therefore, it is natural, to think that the focus of what Hospice does is on death. But healing can have different meanings beyond the physical. In fact, our focus in Hospice is not on illness, or on life's finiteness, although these are certainly realities.

Samuel Beckett in his play, *Waiting for Godot*, elegantly characterizes the phenomenology of life: "Down in the hole, lingeringly, the gravedigger puts on the forceps, we have time to grow old." Life's finiteness is not the province only of Hospice patients; it is the existential condition of all our lives. The only difference is that most hospice patients are suddenly faced with that reality; for many of them, death is now real, life, therefore, becomes precious and life's priorities become foreground.

LIFE REVIEW

Beyond the physical, there are the spiritual and emotional/psychological aspects of healing that the Hospice seeks to influence. An aspect of this healing lies within the patients' natural tendency to review their lives. The histories that patients relate are stories of their lives and, like all stories, they have beginnings, middles, and, now, ends. There are various characters that weave in and out of the tales. Some are peripheral to the patients' stories; other characters have impacted the patients in life-altering ways. It is the clinician's responsibility to help the clients make useful meaning of their life stories.

In the article, "Meaning Construction in Palliative Care," Romanoff and Thompson (2006) state:

> Patients do not tell stories that are an accurate reflection of an objective or factual reality. Rather, narratives are social and linguistic constructions, derived from experience, through which humans shape experience and confer meaning. (p. 310)

Too often, life review is construed as the goal rather than the process. The job of the clinician is to help co-construct with the patient and family a life story that conveys a sense of purpose and meaning. Romanoff and Thompson reflect this sentiment: "Healing is experienced when the narrator can tell a story of illness and loss that gives meaning and purpose to his or her life.... It is the intersubjective telling of the story in the presence of an empathic witness that fosters healing" (p. 311).

It is, therefore, not in the telling of the story but in the co-construction of its meaning wherein healing lies. The processes entail the telling and active listening; the goal is meaning making. Wittgenstein (1958) says, "Language is a labyrinth of paths. You approach from *one* side and know your way about; you approach the same place from another side and no longer know your way about" (p. 82). Active listening involves exploring the yet to be known, and guiding the teller into stories that construct healing.

DENIAL

In the eagerness to prepare the patient and the family for the patient's death, it is often assumed that the goal for the patient and family is to explore and give vent to their thoughts and feelings about some inevitable future. In accord with theories on catharsis, somehow this will lead to acceptance. Our perceived and theorized goal then takes precedence over the patient's and/or the family's goal.

There are times that the patient or family will not acknowledge the impending death. I have sat through too many interdisciplinary team meetings and have heard fellow professionals from many different disciplines characterize such patients as being "in denial." In this context, the meaning is that the patient and his or her family refuse to accept the reality of illness and inevitable demise. However, if healing is to take place, they must.

Elisabeth Kübler-Ross (1969) addresses her concept of denial:

> Denial, at least partial denial, is used by almost all patients not only during the first stages of illness or following confrontation, but also later on from time to time. *I regard it as a healthy way of dealing with the uncomfortable and painful situation with which some of these patients have to live for a long time.* Denial functions as a buffer after unexpected shocking news, allows the patient to collect himself and, with time, mobilize less radical defenses. [Italics added] (p. 39)

"Denial" is something to be respected and understood as useful for the patient and the family at that moment in time. It need not be confronted nor theorized as needing to be dissolved in order for the patient to experience a sense of healing. I would suggest that it is vastly more important for the patient to make useful meaning of his or her life rather than accept death. In my experience, the former often leads to the latter.

The Five Stages

Kübler-Ross' book, *On Death and Dying*, was considered innovative when it was first published in 1969. Someone had actually addressed the remaining socially taboo subject, death. The concept of five stages – denial, anger, bargaining, depression, and acceptance – was a useful guideline to help normalize the dying experience.

Since its publication, it has been common to interpret Kübler-Ross' words to mean that one could not reach a state of acceptance without going through the stages sequentially. Kübler-Ross did not explicitly state this; however, just using the term "stages" in and of itself can serve to reinforce this belief. *The Oxford Desk Dictionary and Thesaurus* (Abate, ed., 1997) defines stage as the "point or period in a process or development."

Benton (1978) reflects that there may have been better choices of words, "That it has been suggested that the various stages be accepted as different *types* of responses or different forms of coping, when death is imminent" (p. 83).

Not only is the term misleading, but also Kübler-Ross' own words lend credence to the idea of a sequential progression[1]:

> These means [sic] will last for different periods of time and will replace each other or exist at times side by side. (p. 122)

And:

> The final acceptance has been reached by many patients without any external help, others needed assistance in working through these different stages in order to die in peace and dignity. (p. 236)

In reviewing the literature (Benton, 1978; Byock, 1997; Kübler-Ross, 1975; Pattison, 1977), it is evident that many writers do not interpret Kübler-Ross' words to mean that the patient and family must work through distinct stages. Pattison (1977) wrote:

> Now, it should be noted that Kübler-Ross did not present these stages of dying as an ineluctable process. A careful reading of her book will reveal that she gives many illustrations where these stages were not followed. Nevertheless, many people quickly concretized her clinical sequence into hard fact. And soon there were many references in the literature to the stages of dying, as if this sequence were really so for most dying persons. (p. 304)

In her last book co-authored with David Kessler (2005), Kübler-Ross acknowledged this interpretation:

> The stages have evolved since their introduction, and they have been very misunderstood over the past three decades. They were never meant to help tuck messy emotions into neat packages. They are responses to loss that many people have, but there is not a typical response to loss, as there is no typical loss. *Our grief is as individual as our lives.*
>
> The five states – denial, anger, bargaining, depression and acceptance – are a part of the frame work that makes up our learning to live with the one we lost. They are tools to help us frame and identify what we may be feeling. *But they are not stops on some linear timeline in grief.*

---

[1] We should put this exploration in its proper context. Kübler-Ross was a pioneer in the field of thanatology. As in any new field, over time the ideas are researched and refined and evolve.

Chapter 6 Stories of Healing: Solution Focus and the Dying Patient

Not everyone goes through all of them or goes in a prescribed order. [Italics added] (p. 7)

As with the concept of denial, there is the danger that the progression through the stages of death becomes the practitioner's goal, not necessarily the patient's or family's. By focusing on what the patient and significant others theoretically *must* do, we miss learning how each individual calls into play his or her own resources and unique ways of making meaning of this experience. It is the patient and family that must ultimately decide what will be the most helpful to them. Only they can decide the journey they wish to take together. Our job is to guide the process, not dictate it.

Solution focus is a compass that will help the patient and significant others to choose their own direction. It provides the tools and philosophical assumptions for the clinician, patient, and family that help develop and maintain meaningful goals, as well as imbue the process with a sense of hope for the future – even in anticipation of death and loss.

Stories of Healing

Barbara and Mike: A Tale of Strength, Courage and Determination[2]

Barbara is 32 years old; her husband Mike is 35. They have two daughters, ages 1 and 5. They had known each other for 18 years and had been married for the past 11. Mike works for a large medical practice as their information systems manager.

Barbara was diagnosed with ovarian cancer about one year ago. She had been undergoing chemotherapy but learned that the cancer spread to her liver. When Barbara called to arrange the appointment with me, she expressed her desire that Mike learn to express his feelings about her diagnosis, deteriorating health, and eventual death. She continued that she didn't feel she was ready for Hospice yet since she was determined to "fight" and would continue in treatment.

When they arrived, it was clear that the disease had seriously affected Barbara physically. She walked slowly, as if each step took much effort and she was rail thin with a gray pallor. They showed me a picture of Barbara prior to her illness. The woman in the picture was a vibrant,

---

[2] All names and other identifying information have been altered.

healthy young woman – a clear contrast to the woman who sat before me that day.

I asked them how our work together might be useful for them. Barbara repeated her concern for her husband and how unprepared he is for the illness and the possibility of her death. Mike began by expressing his skepticism. He said that he had been willing to come because it was Barbara's wish that he do so, but that he didn't "believe in psychology" and didn't think that the session could be helpful.

I asked them the Miracle Question and he responded that he would be "at peace with God." I asked him to expand on this and he replied that he would have short-term goals and organize the family. He continued that he would make plans for the care of his daughters and become both mother and father to them if the future required it. Mike said that while his employer has given him assurances, he fears for his job since he concentrates more on Barbara than he does on his work. I asked him how the miracle might make that different and he replied that he would have confidence that the future is "in God's hands" and this would give him a sense of peace and security. This, in turn, would help him to concentrate better.

Barbara said that she would know that her family is secure and will be provided for. She especially hoped that Mike would continue to live with their daughters in the house that they both had built together. I asked her what would be the very first thing she would do tomorrow – the morning after the miracle happened. Without hesitation and to my surprise (and I think to Mike's as well), she replied that she would do several things: pick out the dress she is to be buried in, go with Mike to choose her casket, and talk to both his and her parents about their assistance in caring for the children once she is gone. I wondered how this might make a difference for her and she replied that she would have a greater sense of her own peace and could better face her illness knowing that she had planned for her husband's and children's future.

I asked them where they would place themselves on a scale where ten is the miracle. They both replied five. Barbara reasoned that it was because she is still alive; they have a good income and shelter. Mike repeated that he was that high on the scale because he knew that things were in God's hands. I then asked them to scale their relationship given what they are now going through together. Barbara replied that she saw things at a six because she wants to continue in her role as mother and wife to the extent that she is able. She said that even though it is increasingly difficult for her, she is still capable of continuing in her role with

Mike's help. Mike replied that he saw their relationship at a ten. He continued that because of Barbara's illness, he has come to recognize what is special about his wife that he had taken for granted.

I asked them to excuse me so I could take some time to think about our conversation. When I returned, I told Barbara that I found her courage and her strength to be inspirational. I shared how I could understand Mike when he spoke about recognizing how special she really is. I told Mike that I, too, was not sure how meeting with me would be helpful, and only time would tell. I continued that I was impressed with how much he cares for Barbara and complimented his unwavering faith in God, despite how this awful disease has ravaged his beloved wife. I said that I was further impressed with Barbara's clarity about what needs to happen in the near future to ensure that her husband and daughters will be provided for and will allow her to better face her illness. I suggested that Mike might want to continue taking notice of those special things about his wife and, further, how this improves his ability to concentrate on his work.

I asked whether they wanted to return for another appointment. Much to my surprise, Mike readily agreed. He must have noticed my reaction and added that he found my focus on the future was helpful to him and was very different than what he had expected. I asked them when they wanted to return and they decided to set another appointment about one month later.

The next day the director of admissions called me to let me know that Barbara had decided to request Hospice services and had been admitted. The Hospice social worker who continued to work with Barbara and Mike informed me that the day after I met with Barbara, she and Mike went together to choose her casket. She also instructed Mike about the dress that she wanted to be buried in, and contacted her parents and in-laws. They committed to helping Mike and the children.

Barbara died peacefully at home surrounded by her loving family less than two months later. I contacted Mike to offer my condolences and spoke about his wife's courage, determination, and strength. Mike expressed his appreciation for my help and referred back to our one session together, stating that it was had been helpful to him.

Discussion: I initially intended to help both Barbara and Mike negotiate their respective goals. I did not assume that they needed to be more realistic about her illness and come to accept that Barbara was a terminal patient. I attempted to listen carefully and respond only to what they wanted to be different. From there I helped them to explore the possibilities and details of the difference and make as useful meaning of their journey together as possible.

In reviewing the case (now some three years later), I am taken with how the Miracle Question, at first blush so seemingly speculative, can lead to such concrete responses. I can only deduce that Barbara and Mike were wise and had a sense of the question's purpose. In doing so, they owned the question and made it useful. For better or worse, words are father to action. The thrust of solution focus is on a conversation that allows useful deeds to result from useful words.

Tom, Marie, Tommy, and Trudy: A Sense of Peace

The Hospice social worker, Lisa Filocco, received a call from Marie, who was concerned that in the midst of an argument, 10-year-old Tommy said to his ill father, "I hope you die" to which Tom replied, "You won't have to worry, I'll be dead soon." Marie expressed the concern that "everything is breaking down." According to Marie, the issue was not only with Tommy, but she and her husband were also in a conflicted relationship. Marie had confided that had it not been for the illness, she and her husband would have been separated and probably divorced a long time before. According to Marie, the major area of conflict was the interference of Tom's family – especially his grandmother – and Tom's refusal to "stand up to them." She further complained that Tom's family neither acknowledged nor respected her roles as wife and mother.

Marie complained that Tom's interactions were usually laced with sarcasm and he was making decisions without consulting her. Lisa had met with the family a few days before the call and she recalled that it did not go well, "They were yelling and screaming at each other." Lisa suggested that they meet as a family and Marie readily agreed. Lisa had recently engaged in a solution focus training and was therefore fairly new to the approach. When she asked for my advice on how to work with the family, I simply suggested she work solution focused, applying what she has already learned.

Lisa had met privately with Tom prior to the family session and suggested that he think about what he would like to be different. Tom is diagnosed with a progressive and untreatable neurological disorder. He replied, "I want to die in peace." Lisa asked him to think about how they might accomplish that and what he would want to say to his family. Lisa

Chapter 6 Stories of Healing: Solution Focus and the Dying Patient   115

arranged with Marie for a time when everyone would be together. Besides their son, Tom and Marie also have an 11-year-old daughter, Trudy.

It would be an understatement to say that the children were reluctant participants. Given their previous session, that would make perfect sense. Tommy sat playing with a video game while Marie exhorted him to stop with little effect. As Marie began to escalate her demand, Lisa interrupted and began the discussion.

Lisa: *Assuming our time together today is useful, when I walk out this door, how will you know that? What needs to happen for you to say, "Wow! That helped"?*

Tommy: Mommy wouldn't be screaming anymore, Mommy wouldn't be crying anymore, Mommy wouldn't be yelling anymore.

Lisa: *So, if Mommy weren't doing all those things, what would she be doing instead?*

Tommy: She just wouldn't be yelling. She wouldn't be the crazy Mommy.

Trudy: We would be spending more time together as a family.

[Marie was tearful and began to complain that the family does not appreciate what she does. Lisa interrupted.]

Lisa: [To Marie] *So, how would you know that our time together was useful?*

Marie: They would respect me more and I wouldn't have to ask them to do something 20 times.

Tom: There would be peace in the family and we would be spending more time together.

Lisa: *All right, spending more time together as a family, a sense of peace... How would you know that these things were happening and how would it make a difference for you?*

Tommy: Mommy wouldn't be yelling and crying.

Marie: [Tearfully] Well, if you want that nice Mommy...

Lisa: *What would she be doing?*

Tommy: She would be talking nicer to me.

Lisa: *Okay, so how would that make a difference for you?*

Tommy: I'd want to come out of my room more and spend time with everyone.

Trudy: I like spending time with the family and watching TV together. We would be closer as a family.

Marie: I guess I would feel more valued by everyone and I think I would feel less stress.

Tom: I know that it would make a difference for my wife. I think it would give me a sense of peace; I especially need that now.

Lisa: *Good, you have some things you want to be different: a sense of peace, feeling closer as a family, spending more time together. Let's suppose that you go to sleep tonight and some miracle happened, but you don't know the miracle happened. You wake up and all these things we were talking about started to happen – more the way you would like them to be. And you didn't know that it happened. What would be going on; how would you know?*

Trudy: We would be together watching TV and we would be talking nice with each other.

Marie: I agree. We would be together talking with each other.

Tom: Not only would we be watching TV together, we would actually be eating dinner together like we used to. Maybe we would play some games.

[The family began to have a lively discussion about how they could arrange to eat dinner together as a family. In the midst of this conversation, Tommy interjected.]

Tommy: [Sarcastically] Yeah, one big happy family.

Marie: See, this is what happens, you try to help and all you get is sarcasm...

Lisa: *Mom, wait. We could easily sit here and spend a lot of time complaining about what we don't want. I'm not sure how that will be helpful. Maybe we can spend time talking about what's working.*

Marie: I just want some respect and less sarcasm.

Tommy: Well, I'm not half as sarcastic as Dad!

[It was clear to Lisa from Tom's reaction that Tommy's comments had hit home. Lisa speculated that Tom might be realizing how much his own sarcasm was affecting the family.]

Lisa: *So, what's the opposite of sarcasm?*
Tommy: Respect.
Lisa: *What does respect look like?*
Tommy: [To Mom] Mommy, I want you to talk nice to me.
Lisa: *Wow, that was great. You can do it! Did you see how Mommy relaxed when you talked to her like that?*
Tommy: Yeah.
Lisa: *You got a very different reaction. You chose to do something different.*

Tommy: You know what else would be different? It would just be the four of us; we wouldn't have all these strangers coming into the house.
Tom: Who do you mean, you mean all our relatives?
Tommy: Yeah, I know they're my relatives but I just wish we could be alone. I don't even know these people!
Marie: He's right. I think for me, if the miracle happened, there would be less interference from Tom's family. They're too involved in our lives. I sometimes think they're taking over.
Lisa: *So let me ask you another kind of question. If I had a scale of 0 to 10, where 10 is the most peaceful you can imagine, and zero is the most chaotic that it has ever been – yelling, screaming, nobody getting along, nobody respecting everybody else…*
Tom: Totally ghetto!
Lisa: *Right. Zero is totally ghetto. Where are you on that scale?*
Tommy: One and a quarter.
Trudy: Five.
Marie: Well some days it's really bad and some days it's not so bad.
Lisa: *Pick a medium, average day.*
Marie: About a three.
Tom: I'd say around five.
Tommy: I want to change mine. I'm going to say three.
Lisa: *Why a three?*
Tommy: Sometimes Mommy does talk nicely to me.
Lisa: *Really? What about you, Trudy?*
Trudy: There are times that we watch movies together and spend time together playing games.
Marie: A week ago, I walked into the room and Tommy and Trudy were playing a game together. Dad even joined them. I think that's why I said three. There has been a time I made dinner and they were more appreciative of it. They even listened to me [she laughs].
Lisa: *How did it make a difference for you when they listened?*
Marie: I felt that they respected me a little bit more – maybe I was more appreciated.
Lisa: *Dad, why five?*
Tom: We are doing some of these things – I just don't think we're doing it enough.
Lisa: *So, what needs to happen so that things will go just one more step on that scale?*

[In general, everyone agreed that being together and having constructive conversations would help raise things on the scale.]

Lisa: So, what else besides these things will bring a greater sense of peace?

Tom: No more sarcasm. I think we have to respect each other and listen to each other more.

[The family decided that it would be a good idea to list all their ideas on a piece of paper. They headed the list with the title "Things that Bring Peace," and created a numbered list of their ideas. As they created their list, the family became much more energized, with everyone participating, shouting out positive ways of achieving peace. As Mom watched this, she began to cry – this time they were very different tears. They agreed that having Lisa return for a follow-up session would be useful.]

Lisa: OK. I want each one of you to notice how the other people in the family are contributing to this sense of peace.

Trudy: Can we write things down?

Lisa: What a great idea! That way you won't miss anything.

[Mom left the room and returned with a notebook for each.]

Tommy: You mean the things we'll know when we get to a five?

Lisa: Right, things you'll know when you get to five.

Lisa received a phone call a week after this session. Marie reported that they had three "wonderful days" immediately following the session. However, the grandmother once again became a central figure for the family. Marie reported that she and Tom reverted back to name calling and a general lack of respect for each other. Lisa offered to meet once again with the family and Marie agreed that a follow-up meeting might be helpful.

When Lisa arrived, both Marie and Tom reported that they had a long talk the previous evening. Marie said that she was able to communicate to Tom how the interference of his family affects her and the family; especially their relationship. According to Marie, Tom acknowledged Marie's concerns and this was something she had "wanted to hear from him for such a long time."

Marie continued that Tom, in fact, spoke with his family and emphatically set limits on their visits, including visiting less often and stating that the family prefers to be together alone for the Thanksgiving holiday. Understandably, Tom's family was not happy about this, but complied with Tom's and the family's wishes. Marie expressed her pride in Tom for taking the position he did and she acknowledged that it took much strength and courage for him to do so.

Chapter 6   Stories of Healing: Solution Focus and the Dying Patient

Tom died on December 30th. Lisa was in contact with Marie after Tom's death. She reported how just after Tom's death, she and the children had become much closer to Tom's family and how they had come to respect and support her.

Discussion: One of the strengths of the solution focused approach is its accessibility. Because there is neither a specialized language nor complicated theory, it is fairly simple to learn. However, as de Shazer (private communication, 1994) stated, "Simple does not mean easy. I'm reminded of the tag line for the board game, Othello, 'Takes a minute to learn and a lifetime to master.'"

It is often assumed that complicated and enduring problems require complicated solutions over long periods of time. Yet, Lisa's intervention began a process that within a brief period of time moved a family from conflicted communication to a greater respect for each other, and an awareness of their boundaries as a family unit.

Although Lisa was relatively new to solution focus, she did a credible job staying focused, listening to the family, and finding ways of utilizing responses that proved useful to the family. By consistently maintaining the focus on their goals stated in positive ways, she moved the family from their usual pattern of sarcasm and conflict to one of cooperation and a sense of positive direction for the future. This is especially seen in Lisa's skillful use of scaling. Lisa readily alters the definition of zero to Tom's tongue-in-cheek suggestion, "totally ghetto." This type of response requires careful listening, and conveys respect for the family's point of view.

While understandably reluctant to participate given their previous experience, Lisa's direction encouraged the children's engagement and active participation. As she takes their input seriously, this further encourages them to be a vital part of the solution picture.

Finally, Marie characterizes Tom's relationship with his family as enduringly enmeshed, and their relationship with her as one of complete disrespect. It has been the source of conflict between the couple and had almost resulted in their separation. There are several related assumptions that we make as solution focused practitioners:

1. A solution need not be related to the problem.
2. Steady state is illusionary – change is inevitable.
3. Change comes from many directions.
4. It doesn't matter where change begins.
5. Once change begins, it tends to lead to more changes (Simon & Nelson, 2007).

After three "wonderful" days as a family, Grandma appears. The family begins to revert to their previous communication style. However, in the midst of this "crisis," Marie and Tom try something different; they calmly discuss the issues. Tom conveyed an understanding of Marie's concerns and, in turn, Marie expressed that she felt respected and heard. But Tom takes it one step further; he confronts his family of origin and tells them that they are to visit less often and not at all during the holiday. Marie is rightfully proud of her husband's new-found strength and courage – especially in the face of a debilitating and terminal illness.

After Tom dies, Marie, Tommy, and Trudy find much solace and support through Tom's family. Their relationship moves in a direction that Marie would probably never have predicted could be possible a short month prior.

One criticism of solution focus that we often hear is that lasting change can only come from changing individuals on a deeper level. Yet by simply staying solution focused, Lisa helped the family make small changes that eventually lead to lasting results. Lisa, together with Tom, Marie, and their family, made meaningful Tom's wish for "a sense of peace."

Mark and Jan: "I Want to Be Remembered."

I received a call from Jan. Her husband, Mark, was diagnosed with esophageal cancer and it appeared that the disease was rapidly progressing. He had recently been under treatment, but the results indicated that the treatment was ineffective. They were considering Hospice but Jan said she was not sure that they were ready yet to accept that Mark's condition was truly terminal.

Jan requested a session stating that there were a number of things they needed to think about, including what would be best for their five-year-old daughter, Emily. I agreed to meet them at their home since Mark was unable to be transported because of his health. I told them of my usual practice of taking a break and asked that they think about where I might go in the house to sit alone for a few minutes and think about our conversation together.

When I arrived, both Mark and Jan were sitting on the couch together. Mark, although weakened by the illness, was nonetheless fully aware and able to actively participate in our conversation. At the time of my visit, Emily was in school.

Chapter 6 Stories of Healing: Solution Focus and the Dying Patient **121**

Jan was a full-time mother; Mark was employed by a large insurance company and was able to continue to work from his home. They both were originally from New Jersey where both their families of origin continued to live. Jan expressed that she planned to return to her hometown since she and Emily would enjoy the support of both her family and Mark's.

I asked them the Miracle Question. Jan responded that she wanted Mark to be able to express his feelings about his illness and impending death.[3] In response, Mark stated that since he has come to accept his condition and demise, he did not feel that expressing his thoughts and feelings would be particularly helpful or necessary. He did say that his major concern is that his daughter would forget about him. He continued that while he expected and wanted his wife to find someone else with whom to share her life ("she's too young to be alone"), his miracle would be that Emily would remember him after he is gone.

I asked Jan how she would know that talking about his feelings would be helpful to Mark. She replied that she was not sure how it would be helpful, but insisted that this was something that she believed he needed to do.

As we discussed his goal, Mark said that he was attempting to spend as much time with his daughter as possible while still physically able. He talked about his love for his daughter and how they had "adventures" together when he was healthy. He described that there were various adventures, including walks through the woods or going to special places, like parks or fairs. I asked whether they had souvenirs of their adventures and he replied that they would often bring a camera and take pictures.

I asked him to scale how confident he was right now that Emily would remember him many years from now. He put himself around a 6 or 7, saying that he had been determined not to be an absent father and to make sure that he took time to be with his daughter since she was born. He referred back to the adventures that he and Emily shared together and spoke about how those were special times for both of them. Finally, he knew that his family would remain actively involved in supporting and caring for Emily and they would help keep his memory alive.

---

[3] This scenario is often repeated in the course of this work. The goal is often expressed that the dying patient needs to talk about his or her feelings (usually it's the woman who feels that the man needs to talk about his death and share his thoughts and feelings). When asked, there usually is no useful end that this would serve. It's another example of how the process is mistaken for the goal. For a further exploration of the role of emotions in SFBP, the reader is referred to Chapter 4 in this book, as well as Simon & Nelson, 2007, pp. 72 & 73; Miller & de Shazer (2000); and de Shazer et al. (2007), pp. 143–151, 154, & 155.

I asked to take the break and returned to affirm their relationship and the support of their respective extended families. I talked about Mark's acceptance of his condition, his love for his daughter and desire that he continues to live in her memory. I said that since he and Emily had gone on many adventures together, that he had already paved the way for what he desired. I suggested that perhaps he and Emily could sit together, remember and create a scrapbook of their adventures. I explained that they could use the photographs they had taken and maybe Emily could draw pictures of their adventures to put in the scrapbook. Mark thought that this seemed like a good suggestion.

Mark and Jan called Hospice the next day and Mark was admitted to the program. Mark died almost exactly one month later. Jan and Emily did return to New Jersey not long after that.

Discussion: I realize that this was the second case presentation in which the patient and their significant other originally did not think they were ready for Hospice and yet called Hospice the day following the session. I want to make clear that I don't define my role as convincing people of the realities of their situations and, therefore, they should avail themselves of Hospice services. In more traditional circles, the term "denial" would no doubt be bandied about. I do think that there is a relationship between having a solution focused conversation, which focuses on the patient's and family's goals and hopes for the future, and their respective acceptance of Hospice services.

Solution focused conversations around end-of-life issues can lead to very practical results. The goal of Hospice intervention is to help the patient co-construct the meaning of his life and how he wants to spend the rest of his days in ways that have meaning for him and his family.

Mark found little need in the expression of feelings for the pure sake of expression. However, he was able to view the meaning of his life and death through the eyes of Emily. For Mark, whatever may lie beyond the River Styx, immortality surely resides within Emily's remembrances.

Warren and Isabel: "The Final Letters"

Warren is a well-known local artist, as well as a carpenter who specializes in fine finishing work. He lives with his wife of 18 years and they have two teen-aged daughters, Kari and Theresa, ages 14 and 16, respectively. Warren had been diagnosed with cancer and was admitted to Hospice after several years of treatment with no improvement and showing a steady decline.

Chapter 6 Stories of Healing: Solution Focus and the Dying Patient

The social worker assigned to Warren and his family was Lisa. When Lisa first met with Warren for the initial assessment, he stated that he was in little pain, and, therefore, had little use for medical intervention, but wanted Lisa to work with him and his family around "improving communications." He continued that since he saw himself as a spiritual person, he needed to find meaning in both his life and his death. Warren admitted that, in general, he had been so busy earning a living pursuing his art career that he had been an absent father. He expressed a hope that he could communicate to his daughters that he loved and cherished both of them very much.

Lisa arranged to meet with the family to discuss their goals for their work together. Isabel complained that her daughters did little to help out in the home, which was becoming an increasing burden because of Warren's failing health. The daughters described their mother as controlling; she never smiled and is "always miserable."

It was clear that Kari and Theresa loved their father, understood the limited time they had together, and wanted to spend as much "quality time" as possible with him. They characterized their father as the proverbial cobbler with the barefoot children, and complained that he started projects in the house but never completed them. They listed their individual bedrooms as well as the family room as examples of projects started but left unfinished. Much of that conversation was around the family room. The girls complained that because there was building material all over the floor, the room was unusable.

Lisa asked them the Miracle Question, ending with the suggestion that all the problems they had been talking about were resolved. Isabel began by saying that the daughters would be helping her without having to be asked. Theresa stated that she would be more amenable to helping her mother because she would be smiling more. Kari said that she would have more of a friendship with her mother and want to spend time with her. Both agreed that their mother would trust them more.

Warren said that he would, in fact, notice that his wife and daughters would be relating better and there would be a greater sense of cooperation and communication in the family. He explained that this was a major concern for him, since after he died he hoped that they would support each other.

Both Kari and Theresa said that they would know that their father loved them. Lisa asked if the miracle did happen and they could know it, what the signs would be. Both girls simply said that their father would finally finish a project that he had started. Lisa asked which room would be the one that Dad would finish on this day after the miracle and they both readily agreed that it would be the family room.

The family expressed appreciation for Lisa's time with them and agreed that the meeting had been productive. They asked her to return for a follow-up session and they all decided to meet the following week.

When Lisa arrived, Theresa and Kari met her at the door and eagerly announced that they were meeting in their completed family room. When Lisa arrived, she found that the floors were now cleared and the room had, indeed, been finished. They told her that because their father was too weak to do the work, he directed them and together the mother and two girls completed the room.

Lisa asked how the session might be helpful and the girls replied that they did not want to spend this session complaining, but wanted to focus on what they appreciated about each other. In fact, that is exactly how they used their time together. Reflecting on that session, Lisa recalled how she had little need for intervention, sat back, watched, and marveled at how this family, self-described as dysfunctional, had transformed itself within such a short time.

Just before ending the session, Warren said that he wanted to provide some "tangible" sign of his love for his family and expressed his regret that he was not able to provide for them as much as he wanted to financially and, therefore, "they had to do without." The girls replied that it was not money that they wanted, but just to know that he loved them. Warren decided that he would write a letter to each one of them that they could read after his death. The family decided that further intervention from Lisa was no longer necessary and they could continue this journey together on their own.

Lisa made several more visits with Warren after this last session. She watched as he progressively declined and, at each visit, he admitted that he had not written the letters. Several weeks later, Warren, now confined to his bed, was becoming rapidly more confused and disoriented; Lisa had doubts that the letters would ever be completed.

In late spring, Lisa made a final visit to Warren. As she walked into his bedroom, she noticed that he was asleep and his breathing was labored. Not wanting to disturb him, she prepared to leave when Warren opened his eyes. Contrary to the most recent visits, Lisa described him at that time as fully oriented and at peace. He talked about his death and his wishes for a memorial service after his cremation. He then directed Lisa's attention to his dresser.

On the top were three envelopes that were to be opened after his death; one each labeled for his daughters and the final one for his wife. Warren died a week after Lisa's visit. Lisa contacted Isabel two weeks after Warren's death. Isabel talked about how the letters were so important to the family and how they brought a sense of joy to all of them. Isabel said that although she, Kari, and Theresa miss him, they are doing well and "continue to recognize Warren's presence in many ways."

Discussion: This case is an example of how, when faced with one's finiteness, the individual tends to focus on what are the most important priorities, and which need to be accomplished. Solution focus provides tools that help facilitate this process in very practical ways.

As solution focused practitioners, we understand the usefulness of establishing concrete goals that are possible within the context of the client's life. Warren is naturally unable to make up for what he describes as a life of neglecting his family. Erik Erikson (1950) describes the final stage of human development as one of generativity versus despair. It was Lisa's staying solution focused with the family that helped favor the former over the latter.[4]

Because Lisa remained focused on the difference that makes a difference (Bateson, 1972), the family was able to move beyond their sense of deprivation, regret, and anger at each other. Together they were able to co-construct a new identity based on mutual support and caring that initially would help prepare each other, including Warren, as they together approached his death. This also paved the way for Isabel and her daughters to support each other after.

The shift from the "dysfunctional" family to a system of mutual support occurred within a brief four-month period. Lisa's focus was not on the regrets and despair over the past – the focus is not on what is *not* possible; the focus is on what *is* possible, and from what is possible to what will make a difference in the family's life context. It is because of the recognition that the family is responsible for their own future, and the assumption that they have the capability of controlling the future, that the family is transformed.

CONCLUSION

For the past 16 of my 30 years of professional experience, I have chosen to think, feel, and act within the solution focused language-game. Initially,

---

[4] This is in no way to imply that Erik Erikson was a social constructivist or a solution focused practitioner.

the question I had asked was, "Will this approach work?" Somewhere within that time, the question shifted to, "How will this approach work?" Based upon my own empirical evidence, I assume that solution focus can be applied in every setting that I have had the privilege to work: community mental health, adolescent day treatment, inpatient psychiatric, pain management clinic, and Hospice work (and, I'm sure, many settings that I have not had the privilege to work). It is also my assumption that my responsibility is to create the context for solution focus.

As solution focused practitioners, we use tools that were developed by listening to clients and very often by the clients themselves. Because these tools have been developed through practice rather than theory, each one (pre-session change questions, future questions, the Miracle Question, exception questions, scaling questions, and coping questions) carries a high probability of usefulness. They are essentially tools for co-constructing conversations that will be helpful to the patients and their significant others.

The question, "Will solution focus work?" is not as useful as, "How will solution focus work?" If experience dictates that a solution focus conversation will most likely result in a useful outcome, then we are obliged to answer the latter question.

When I talked to my first dying patient's wife to arrange the first visit, I began with strategizing how I would create the context for solution focus. I informed the wife that I would be doing an assessment as required of me as a social worker. In this context, I would be asking a lot of questions (because assessments require asking a lot of questions). I then said that after I finished gathering all the information I needed, I would want to take a brief break and sit alone so I can sort out the information. Afterward I would meet with the patient and his wife again to share my thinking and whatever suggestions I might have. I asked them to think about a space where I could sit alone for a few moments.

I also told the wife that as part of the process we would need to decide on some goals for our work together. I asked her to confer with her husband and think about how they would know that our work together was being useful to them; this would be the basis of the plan of care. When I did meet with them, and at the point that I thought that the Miracle Question would be useful, I phrased it as a question that I am required to ask as part of the assessment process.[5]

---

[5] This idea was first suggested to me by my colleague Dan Gallagher who would explain to his clients in a drug treatment center that he was required to ask the Miracle Question as part of a research project.

Chapter 6 Stories of Healing: Solution Focus and the Dying Patient   **127**

Once placed in context, the solution focus approach made perfect sense to this family (and subsequent patients and/or families since). As I have gotten better at timing the Miracle Question, I've found that I could more naturally ask it without having to make it part of a regulatory process. Initially, I explained to the social workers learning solution focus that in the beginning it would be natural to feel awkward when first applying the practice. However, patients and their families assume that the practitioner is well trained, educated, and experienced. In that context, patients and families can be expected to make sense of the procedures and questions.

I hope that this chapter has served to convince practitioners that the solution focused brief approach can have very positive results for both patients with life-limiting conditions and their families. As de Shazer et al. (2007) state, "Our job is to create the conditions under which clients find their own solutions, to help clients look into their hearts to find out what they truly want and how they might get there" (p. 156). The purpose of this chapter is to clearly demonstrate that even those who are confronted with the knowledge that their life spans are limited are not exempt from this process.

7 Expect the Unexpected: Solution Focus With a Widowed Client

> Go with me, like good angels, to my end;
> And, as the long divorce of steel falls on me,
> Make of your prayers one sweet sacrifice,
> And lift my soul to heaven.
> —*William Shakespeare,*
> **Henry VIII,** *Act I, Scene 1*

The frequent assumption is that clients see a clinician because they want to heal from the loss of a significant other. After practicing solution focus for over 16 years, I've come to realize that making assumptions about what the client needs or wants may lead into directions that obfuscate rather than clarify. The lesson from this case is that the client's goal is the compass.

I met with Bill in early April of 2006. He called to schedule a bereavement session, stating that his wife of 12 years died of cancer in May, 2005. Initially, I asked him what he does and he replied that he works at the state correctional institution, supervising inmates in a work/study program.

When I asked him where he learned the trade that he teaches, he explained that he had been incarcerated for 27 years in a state correctional institution. While there, he had been involved in a similar program. Bill related the story that one day in prison "a big black guy came up to me and said that he was going before the parole board soon and needed to befriend a white guy in order to impress the board."

Bill described how the fellow inmate chose Bill "after looking around at all the white guys in prison. He said I was the only white guy around who had any sense." Bill described how they became close friends and it was because of this man that Bill became involved in a newly created college degree program while in prison and earned his Bachelors Degree in sociology. Bill was released in 1989 and shortly thereafter was employed by the same institution, teaching other inmates what he had learned.

I asked Bill how he thought our conversation together might be helpful to him and he explained that he had been married prior to his incarceration, and this marriage had ended in what he described as a contentious divorce. He described his second marriage as equally conflicted; however, after experiencing the first divorce, he decided that he would rather endure this relationship than face another devastating divorce.

Other than his job, Bill had few interests and less social support. He reported that he has a sister who has been supportive of him and believed in him despite his incarceration. He said that he has had no contact with the sister for about one year.

A social work intern sat in on my sessions with Bill. A break was taken at the end of each of two sessions; the intern and I consulted before returning with complementary ideas to Bill.

FIRST SESSION

The following are excerpts from the first session:

Joel: *So, what is it that will tell you that meeting with me has been helpful to you?*
Bill: Well, I met my wife through a pen pal program when I was in jail. When I came out, we got married pretty quickly and she pretty much took care of me and organized my life. This is the first time that I've been on my own and I feel like I'm in limbo.
Joel: *What would be happening different from limbo?*
Bill: I would want some kind of life, develop friendships.
Joel: *Okay, what would be the first sign to you that you're having that kind of life?*

Chapter 7 Expect the Unexpected: Solution Focus With a Widowed Client   **131**

Bill: I don't know. [I pause waiting for a response.] I guess I would clean my apartment. Sometimes I feel like I'm living like a slob.

Joel: *Okay, so you'd have some kind of life, maybe develop some friendships. Perhaps you'd clean your apartment. Let me expand a bit on this vision. Bill, I have this strange question. I'd like to get a clearer picture of how we'll know together... well, that we can stop meeting like this.* [He smiles.] *This is a question that I find helpful for doing that. Let's suppose that after we talk today, you're going to go and do your normal things. Tonight you're going to go to sleep. Let's suppose that while you're sleeping, some miracle happens. The miracle is that you've begun to have the kind of life that you want. However, you don't know that this miracle has happened – yet. The only way you can know about this miracle is what's different tomorrow – the small clues. That's my question. How would you know that the miracle happened and this different kind of life has just begun after you wake up tomorrow after the miracle?*

Bill: [Long pause] I guess I would come home and do something after work that I'll feel good about.

Joel: *Like what?*

Bill: [Long pause] I don't know.

Joel: [Another long pause while I wait for him to think about an answer.]

Discussion: Many of Bill's responses are prefaced by "I don't know." This is not unusual. There are different ways of understanding this response. It could be understood as the client being resistant, or uncooperative. It could even be mistakenly understood as a "real" response. One of the behaviors that is common to many language-games is turn taking: one person speaks, waits until the other person responds, then the first person speaks again. de Shazer (personal communication, 1994) likened turn taking to playing tennis. The ball can only be returned when it is in my court. "I don't know" is essentially a nonresponse; the ball remains in the other person's court. An "I don't know" response gives me nothing to respond to.

It may be more useful to think of "I don't know" as the client's attempt to follow the turn-taking rule of the language-game – he or she is just attempting to be polite. Dan Gallagher (Korman, 2004) suggests that perhaps "I don't know" is equal to "Shut up – I need time to think." Solution focused questions are questions that are new to clients and require them to be in a very different language-game. "I don't know" serves two purposes: 1) The response maintains the rule of turn taking, and 2) the response gives the client room to think. It behooves the clinician to respect the client's need for reflection and to wait for a response. Often, the client's internal process of envisioning a better future is as useful as the response.

I have, at times, followed a suggestion given by Insoo Kim Berg (Korman, op. cit.). When "I don't know" seems to be real versus a request for thinking space, I've said to the client, "Suppose you did know, what would you say then?" It is very interesting how most clients will come up with a response. Perhaps it is because they realize that the clinician is convinced that the question is an important one and expects an answer. Another option is to simply state, "Of course you don't know. Guess."

The above exchange is a good example of how a vague but positive response to the initial question, "How might the conversation make a difference?" can be woven into the Miracle Question. Bill responds that he wants "some kind of life." I recognize this as a possible introduction to solution building and, using the Miracle Question, invite him to expand on his vision of the kind of life he wants.

Bill: I guess I would begin to care about myself.
Joel: *Great! Take care about yourself. How would you know that was happening?*
Bill: Maybe I would get out of the house and start doing something with my time, rather than just sitting in front of a TV after I get home.
Joel: *So, this miracle happens and tomorrow you're doing that. You come home after work, maybe have some supper, and then you go out. Where to?*
Bill: Maybe just going to a gym or joining a club with other people – something like that.
Joel: *Let's suppose that you do that. How do you think that it'll make a difference in your life?*
Bill: I don't think that I'd feel as much in a rut as I do now. Maybe I would begin to enjoy my life just a little bit and think that I'm more than just an ex-con. Maybe I'd figure out that I can take care of myself.
Joel: *Right, right. Let's do this; suppose I had a scale from 0 to 10, where 10 is you really care about yourself. Where would you put things right now?*
Bill: Oh, below zero.

Chapter 7 Expect the Unexpected: Solution Focus With a Widowed Client

Joel: Below zero. Okay. let's tweak the scale a bit. Let's suppose it were a minus five to a plus five scale, where would you put yourself then?
Bill: Minus four.
Joel: Minus four – How come not minus five?
Bill: Well, at least I don't think about suicide.
Joel: Well, that's a good thing! What do you think about instead?
Bill: [Laughs] Not much – I guess that's why I watch TV so much.
Joel: What would you be thinking about instead?
Bill: I suppose going out and doing something that's fun.
Joel: Okay. So if things went up just a little bit to a minus three, how would you know?
Bill: I would be cleaning my apartment.
Joel: Cleaning your apartment. That sounds like something important to you. How will it make things different?
Bill: I guess I would just feel more organized – it would help me get motivated maybe. I get home tired, and I guess depressed, and I don't want to do anything except stare off at the boob tube.

Discussion: It is not usual for a response similar to Bill's "below zero." My thinking here is to follow the adage that no matter what the client responds, my job is to assume it can be useful and then to use it. In another case, when I asked a client a zero-to-ten scale, she responded that she was at a minus five. I asked her why not a minus six. My assumption was that she wanted to change the scale and I was obliged to cooperate with her.

In Bill's case, I heard his response as an indication that we must be using a different scale than zero to ten, and, therefore, changed the scale to minus five to plus five. It appears that this was better for him because he placed himself within that scale. In turn, this gave us a chance to co-construct exceptions and future possibilities. The lessons here are that scaling needs to be flexible, meet the needs of the client, and the numbers have no meaning until the client and the therapist together co-construct a meaning, which can be better or worse depending on the direction of the conversation.

Joel: Bill, let me do another one of those scales, okay? [He nods.] Let's say ten is that you're so disgusted with the way things are, you're going to go home today and do something about it. Where would you put yourself?
Bill: Three.

Joel: *How come three?*
Bill: I don't like where I am right now. I know I need to do something.

Discussion: I could have had ten stand for "you're going to go home today and do something about it." I wonder how that would have differed from setting the scale with the idea that he is so disgusted with the way things are, that he will take action. This is a wonderfully paradoxical scale. It places the problem and Bill's disgust with the problem at ten. It can be thought of as ten is "you are disgusted and you are going to do something about it," and zero is "you are disgusted and you are going to do nothing about it." The fact that he places himself above zero (at three) suggests strongly that there is some probability that he is likely to take some action.

Joel: *Bill, I have one more of those scales before we take a break and think about our conversation together.* [The social work intern] *and I are probably going to come up with a suggestion – something to think about or try. Where would you put things where ten is that you would do any crazy suggestion we might come up with – as long as it's legal, no one gets hurt, and it won't cost you anything – to make things better.*
Bill: Seven.
Joel: *Wow, okay. That's pretty high! How come?*
Bill: I know I have to do something – I can't keep living like this.
Joel: *Well I'm going to take that break and think about things for a while. Is there anything else you feel you need to tell us, or anything specifically that you want us to talk about?*
Bill: No.

Discussion: It is interesting to trace the evolution of the goal in this first session. Bill begins the session unclear about how he wants things to be different. In fact, he tells us that his wife organized his life and he feels directionless without her. As the session progresses, he becomes clearer that he perceives that he needs to take some action, and there is even some clarity about what that action might be. The former is far more important than the latter. I have no idea what action Bill might take. I do think that as a result of our conversation, the probability of his taking some action has significantly increased.

Joel: [*Returns from the break.*] *Well, we were really impressed how you turned your life around. Here you were in prison, met some*

Chapter 7   Expect the Unexpected: Solution Focus With a Widowed Client   135

guy who thought you were the only white guy around who had any sense. You went into the college program, earned a degree, and learned a trade. You're working full time now supervising inmates.

It made sense to us that now you have the challenge of learning to live on your own. You were in prison where they told you when to sleep, when to wake, when to eat, when to breathe. Then you left and married someone who also took care of you. It seemed to us that you know how to be organized since you have to do that on your job [he nods in agreement]. *It also seemed to us that your problem is trying to figure out how to do at home what you're already doing on your job. For now, our suggestion is that you don't change anything, yet, but just notice what happens that tells you that, in fact, things could improve.*

[Bill agrees to return and an appointment is set for one week later.]

Discussion: We can outline this feedback using the template suggested in Chapter 5:

- *Normalizing*: "You were in prison where they told you when to sleep, when to wake, when to eat, when to breathe. Then you left and married someone who also took care of you."
- *Restructuring*: "It made sense to us that now you have the challenge of learning to live on your own." The problem is not that he is unable to organize his life; the problem is that he needs to figure out how to do at home what he can already do on the job.
- *Affirmation of Competencies*: He knows how to be organized (he does it on the job), he graduated college while incarcerated, he learned a trade, he impressed another inmate as the "only white guy who had any sense," and he is working full time.
- *Suggestion*: This suggestion – just notice what indicates that things could improve – is a classic example of going more slowly than the client. In discussing the suggestion during our break, the intern and I agreed that it would not be useful to suggest something that would push Bill faster than he is willing to go. We discussed that many of the ideas that arose from the session represented new thinking for Bill and he needed time to think about the conversation. We also thought that it was important for him to control his progress and, therefore, actualize his own goal: taking control over his life.

SECOND SESSION

I begin the second session with Bill.

Joel: So, what's better even a little bit?
Bill: I cleaned up the kitchen.
Joel: Really? So how did that make a difference to you?
Bill: Oh, I do that about once a month when I can't stand it any longer. I guess I have a motivation problem.
Joel: A motivation problem. How would you know that this was different?
Bill: I don't know. [Long pause] Because [when] I was in prison, my wife saw me as a low life and thought that she needed to save me. We were married for 12 years. You know, people who know me can't believe that we slept in the same bed and never touched each other for the past ten years.
Joel: So, how will you know that things are getting better?
Bill: I don't know. Well, I return from work and I have no friends and I don't do anything.
Joel: I'm not sure; is that something that you want to change or something that you think you should change? How much of what you're doing – going to work, going home – are you content with?

Discussion: I thought after the previous session that Bill and I were clearer about the goal. This prior interchange is a way of making sure that we are on the same page. One of the key questions here is whether having friends is something he wants to do, or something he thinks he should do.

Bill: I don't know. My wife took away my self-esteem.
Joel: How would you know that this was different – that you had your self-esteem back?
Bill: [Long pause] I would change something in the living room.
Joel: How would that make a difference?
Bill: [There's a long pause, tears begin to well up in his eyes. Soon he is sobbing, hugging himself, and rocking back and forth. The intern and I sat quietly during this, patiently waiting.]
Joel: Changing something in the living room seems to be important to you.
Bill: I would feel like I'm making something my own.
Joel: What do you mean?

Bill: Well, my wife saw me as a low life, a project for her to work on. It was really her house; she wouldn't let me touch anything or change anything – I was just not good enough. I don't know – I guess just changing something would make me feel like the place was beginning to be mine.

Discussion: The goal is less important than the meaning of the goal – how will it make a difference? How will it change the way the client thinks, feels about himself, and how will it change his behavior in positive and meaningful ways? The action is simple: changing things in the living room. For Bill, it can have profound connotations.

Joel: Bill, let me do one of those crazy scales. How about ten is things are on track for you and you can probably continue on your own without us?
Bill: About a one.
Joel: Really? If my memory serves me, you were at a minus three last week. Is that right?
Bill: Yes.
Joel: So, how did things go from minus three to one?
Bill: I thought about things we talked about last time and I left here feeling a little more hopeful. I especially thought about what you said – that I know how to be organized on the job. I just need to figure out how to do that at home. I guess thinking about changing things at home is a step in that direction.

Discussion: If I could rewind this session, I do not think that I would have added the phrase "and you can probably continue on your own without us." It was likely moving much too fast for Bill. In fact, a scale about being on track when he went from a minus three to one is probably too quick a pace as well. A better question might have been, "What is happening at one that was not happening at minus three?" It might be interesting for the reader to consider other possibilities.

Joel: One more scale before our break. I think I asked you this last week. How about ten means you're willing to do anything?
Bill: I'm willing to do almost anything.
Joel: Great, I'm going to take that break. Anything you need to tell me?
Bill: When I was in jail, I got involved in a program to talk to teenagers about staying out of jail.

Joel: *Really?* [Bill briefly describes that program.]

[After the break.] *You know, I thought that it's paradoxical that jail was really a very productive time for you: you learned a trade, you got a college degree, and you were involved in this counseling program. You really were productive. I bet that your self-esteem was pretty high back then.* [He nods in agreement.]

It seemed to us that you and your wife had very different ideas about what married life should be. She saw you as a low-life and herself as like the Salvation Army, whose purpose is to save you. This will come as no surprise to you – you can't change the past. You know, I have a friend who said to me once, "Joel, I have both bad news and good news. The bad news is that people don't change much. The good news is that people don't need to change much to make a big difference."[1]

You know, I don't believe that people should do something unless it makes a difference for them. We have a suggestion with three periods – we'll let you decide how long a period is. Period one: Spend some time looking around the living room and think about the one or two things that if you changed them, it would probably make a difference for you. Period two: Pick something to change and change it any way that makes sense to you. Period three: Notice how the change makes a difference for you. If it doesn't make a difference, go back and start again. [He is handed a printed copy of the suggestion.]

Okay, we can either pick another time when you think you'll have done the suggestion and have something to tell us, or you can call when you're ready.

Bill: I already know what I'm going to do. I was thinking about it during the break.

Joel: *Really, what?*

Bill: I'm going to rotate the mattress.

Joel: *Rotate the mattress. What would that mean to you?*

Bill: Well, she would never rotate the mattress because she didn't want me sleeping on her side of the bed. If I did that it would finally make the bed mine. I thought about something else I should do.

Joel: *Really, what is that?*

Bill: Remember I told you about having a pen pal in prison? Well, I first started to write to a female friend, Linda, who lives in Texas. In

---

[1] That friend was my first instructor in the Ericksonian training, Father James Warnke.

fact, she told my wife about me and that got my wife to write me also – that's sort of how we first met. Once I got out of jail, I finally met Linda face-to-face. We actually had a brief affair. I'm thinking that I should travel out to meet Linda again. Who knows what might happen.

Joel: *Sounds like a plan. So, what do you want to do about another appointment?*

Bill: You gave me a lot to think about and I have some ideas of what I should do. I'll give you a call when I'm ready.

Joel: *Great.* [We all stand up and Bill shakes my hand.]

Bill: You know, this is the first time I've opened up to anyone like this. I really felt like you listened and didn't judge me. Thank you.

Joel: *It is I that thank you!*

This was the last session with Bill. He was one of those surveyed two years later as part of the outcome survey reported in Chapter 6. When asked to scale progress in question one of the survey, he placed himself at a four.

Discussion: The clinician truly does not know what to expect when he or she enters into the solution-building process – this is what makes solution focus so interesting; every client is unique. Even the smallest and seemingly most insignificant goal can be co-constructed to make a big difference in a client's life. Bill sought bereavement counseling not necessarily because he grieves for his wife, but because of the loss of what he views as the organizing principle in his life. The conversation serves to deconstruct this frame and begins a process of re-constructing his competence, and a new direction. There is the hint of this when he reports that he left the first session with hope. For Bill, it is not just a mattress and living room that he changes. In those very acts, he makes the bed his own, he makes his house his own, and he makes his life his own.

8 The Other Woman: Solution Focus With a Bereaved Family

> The quality of mercy is not strained,
> It droppeth as the gentle rain from heaven
> Upon the place beneath. It is twice blest:
> It blesseth him that gives and him that takes.
> —*William Shakespeare,* **The Merchant of Venice,** *Act IV, Scene 1*

Chapter 5 presented outcome data taken from a survey of clients who had been last seen for bereavement sessions at least six months prior to the phone interviews. One session was the single (modal), most frequent, number accounting for 46 percent of the total. This is consistent with psychotherapy outcome data.

The following case is an example of a one-session, solution focused counseling visit. Sharon's two grown children, Robert and Teri, accompanied her. Sharon had been estranged for four years from her husband, Frank. Frank had been diagnosed and died of cancer one year prior to this session.

Sharon had called to arrange a bereavement counseling session after Frank's death, stating that she was concerned about the effect his death has had on her children, and needed guidance on how to best help them. After introductions, I began the conversation.

Joel: *What we're going to do is we're going to talk a little bit. Somewhere along the line, after I run out of questions (that takes me a long time* because I get curious), I'm going to take a break. I'm going to go off by myself, review my notes, think about our conversation, write some ideas down, maybe a suggestion – something to think about, notice, experiment with. Come back and share that with you. So, Mom, what do you do?*

Sharon: I work as a nursing instructor [at a local college]. I worked many years as an oncology nurse before: cancer treatment, transplants, those sorts of things.

Joel: *So, how long have you been teaching college?*

Sharon: Five years.

Teri: Wow, I didn't realize that it was that long!

Joel: *Time goes fast. Teri, what do you do?*

Teri: I go to school now. I'm going to apply to medical school – just finishing up the classes.

Joel: *Just starting to apply?*

Teri: Yeah. I'll apply this summer for next school year. My undergraduate degree was in business.

Joel: *Wow! So what made you go from business to medicine?*

Teri: I don't know. I guess I just had a change of heart.

Joel: *Anything to do with your dad?*

Teri: Probably, that probably had some influence on it. It was not too long after that – maybe a year. I was working and it was kind of boring.

Joel: *And Robert, what do you do?*

Robert: I'm a student. Right now I'm not doing much. I took a year and went down to Australia to live with my girlfriend. Now I'm going back to college in the fall.

Joel: *Studying what?*

Robert: International relations.

Joel: *How long were you in Australia?*

Robert: Eight months.

Joel: *Eight months. So when did you come back?*

Robert: About a month ago. I was going to go to school down there, but it really wasn't working out for me. So I decided to come back and finish my degree up here.

Joel: *What made you decide to come back?*

Robert: The education down there wasn't so great and I wasn't feeling so well.

Joel: *[To everyone] Interests, hobbies, things that you enjoy doing?*

Teri: Um, shopping? [All laugh.] Going to the gym.

Chapter 8   The Other Woman: Solution Focus With a Bereaved Family

Sharon: That's Teri! Having had all this happen, I'm kind of introverted – preparing my lectures, trying to do this and trying to do that. For a while, I was doing ballroom dancing. I found I just didn't have the energy or the will to dress and go out. I did it for about two years, but I haven't done it in a while.
Joel: Something you enjoyed?
Sharon: Yeah. I love to dance. I've always been a dancer.
Joel: Great! Robert?
Robert: I like bicycling a lot. I'll probably go four or five times a week.
Joel: Where do you go?
Robert: All around. Where I live has a lot of windy hills. I also like cooking and trying new foods. I'm trying to cook more.
Joel: Is he a good cook?
Sharon: Oh, yes!
Joel: What kind of stuff do you cook?
Robert: Simple stuff, really, but I try new things.

Discussion: There are several reasons that I begin sessions with questions about the family members' lives and interests. It suggests that this is about them and what they know about themselves – their areas of expertise, strengths, and resources. When the clinician demonstrates an interest in the client, it helps to facilitate a working relationship.

One of the misconceptions of many of the psychodynamic theories of psychotherapy is that therapeutic bonding requires a long-term relationship. Research actually suggests that the clinical bond and therapy duration are not connected (Miller et al., 1997). My experience suggests that the bond is developed through an interest and respect in the client and what he or she says.

Many (if not most) clients were involved in activities prior to the death of the loved one that provided them with a sense of accomplishment and satisfaction. It is not unusual for clients, as in Sharon's case, to talk about such activities and to suggest that reestablishing those very activities are important elements in the healing process. Knowing more about clients' interests, hobbies, activities, family, and social supports are important factors in assessing and eventually co-constructing resources.

Joel: [To Sharon] *I asked you a question and asked you to share that with Teri and Robert.*
Sharon: I did.

Joel: *So, presuming our time together is useful, how will you know – maybe later today or tomorrow?*

Sharon: I think it would be helpful to me if... see, my husband died – we had separated. Still, we got along; he came up and visited the kids. We remained very friendly. Then he met this woman who, as far as I'm concerned, didn't like that and pulled him away. Then he got cancer – he was diagnosed in April of 2006. He died in October. There was a big scene with this woman at the hospital. She wanted to take over his treatment, his funeral arrangements from his family – even though we were divorced. And that was including his own mother. So, when I think about it and his death, I'm very disappointed that instead of being there with him, and supporting him, we had this woman who was just... I mean to the point of the staff calling her [by his last name]. She even wrote the obituary because we were so distraught. She put in it that she was his fiancée. That was news to us. We are a close family, and it's been a struggle ever since. When I think about that, I feel bad inside. I think about being down there – it was a bad scene. As far as I'm concerned, she wasn't nice to Robert. She was okay with Teri. I could tell you stories about this situation that would make your toe nails curl. I think to myself that I wish that hadn't happened; I could have gone in and held his hand. I wish I could have concentrated more on the situation and taking care of him. So he died in October. His mother was supposed to come down for Teri's birthday in January but she never showed. We called and called her. Teri finally called the police and they saw her on the floor in the kitchen. She had had a massive stroke.

Teri: She was very independent.

Sharon: She just got back from Egypt. She went everywhere. She was taken to the hospital but she kept getting worse. They didn't think she was going to make it. She lived but her whole left side is paralyzed – she doesn't even know that she has a left side. She is in rehabilitation now. So, Teri lost her father, and then her grandmother got sick. Robert is not around. Both Robert and I got depressed. Teri is not as prone to depression as Robert and I are.

Joel: *A lot has happened in such a short time. So if things were different and this was helpful, how would you know?*

Discussion: Even after introducing the pre-session question that essentially asks how life would be better once the problem is solved, it is not unusual for clients to detail all the problems that they are experiencing.

Chapter 8   The Other Woman: Solution Focus With a Bereaved Family

Sharon's response is a virtual smorgasbord for a problem-solving language-game and an invitation to co-construct the problems associated with Frank's abandonment and death. My response is first to acknowledge the changes, and then to refocus on how things will be different if the conversation proves useful.

Sharon: I think if it were helpful, I could somehow overcome the feelings that I have about that situation, and begin to remember him as a good husband, and how he was a good father to my children, instead of always thinking about this thing that's going on.

Joel: *That would be the sign to you – that you could remember him as a good father and a good husband?*

Sharon: Right.

Joel: *What pieces of that would you be remembering?*

Sharon: I would be remembering if I had to write down qualifications for a wonderful husband and a wonderful father, he would fit every aspect of that.

Joel: *Tell me about that. What would you be writing down?*

Sharon: This comes to my mind first. He had so much fun even when they were little. When Teri was first born, his job was to bathe her. I was nursing her so he had to do something. Then he would love to take her out for lollipops and newspapers. Get up early in the morning, put on her snowsuit, and take her out. Of course, he did the same to Robert. There wasn't a soccer team, or a basketball team, or a little league team that he didn't coach. He'd get up early in the morning and make their lunches, and go to every parent/teacher conference. He was just the best father, and he also never had a harsh word with me. We hardly ever argued. He was understanding. I went back to school for nursing when Teri was little. He took care of the kids and balanced that with a job.

Joel: *So, your difference is remembering him as a good father.*

Sharon: I think so.

Discussion: It would be very tempting to define my role (at least in part) as helping Sharon's "reality test" by raising the cognitive dissonance between the ideal vision of her husband versus the fact that he abandoned the family. She states that it would be helpful, and, therefore, her goal is to think of her husband as a good father. I respect and take at face value her frame that this would be helpful. By asking her details of how she would be thinking differently, I help her to actually think differently. This is an example of having a "both/and" conversation rather than an "either/or" conversation (see Chapter 3). She states that overcoming the feelings about the situation would result from thinking differently about it. There is the unspoken implication that she understands that both the positive and negative aspects of the relationship with her husband coexist – it is a question of which one would be the most helpful focus for moving in a useful direction.

Teri: I think what would be the most helpful for me would be whatever would make Mom and Robert the most happy. What would make them feel better.

Joel: *What would tell you that just watching Mom and watching Robert? What would each one be doing or saying?*

Teri: I think they wouldn't be so sad anymore. They would both be able to remember more like how I remember. When I think about it – I mean I don't think about that other woman – maybe I'm blocking it out or something. I think I had more contact with him when he was dying so I don't feel like I'm missing something. I was in the hospital with him almost every day. The other woman was there only the last three days or so. I had more time with him because of that.

Robert: I actually had a lot of time with him also. Even after he left, he would come visit me – I was going to school in Boston. We would go out together and have dinner. He came up one time and, even though he was weak because of the cancer, we went canoeing.

Joel: *So do I get it? That for you, similar to Teri, you would more see the difference with Mom?*

Robert: I think so.

Joel: *What would you both notice about her?*

Robert: That she would overcome the memories of what happened those last few days of Dad's life.

Teri: Yeah, I would agree with that.

[I ask the Miracle Question using Robert's phrase that Mom would "overcome the memories."]

Sharon: You know I was always enthusiastic about life. And even though I didn't get them all done, I had a lot of things in life I was going to do.

Joel: *So if the miracle happened, what would be different about that?*

Sharon: Well, the first thing I would do would go back to dancing. Maybe I would go into the [New York] City and take lessons. I would exercise.

Chapter 8 The Other Woman: Solution Focus With a Bereaved Family

Joel: *Exercise?*

Sharon: I'd get up early and take a nice walk. Maybe I would do something with Teri. Maybe we'd go to the gym together.

Teri: Maybe you'd quit smoking.

Joel: *Quit smoking, okay. What would be the very first thing? The smallest thing that you would notice different?*

Sharon: When I wake up in the morning, I think about what I have to do and I get anxious in my stomach.

Joel: *What would be different?*

Sharon: I would just get up and know what I needed to do and not have that anxious feeling.

Teri: What would make me happy is knowing they were happy. Sometimes I worry about both of them. For me, the most worrisome is just wondering whether Robert is going to be okay. Now that he's home, I feel much better.

Joel: *So hearing Robert talking about going back to college, what difference does that make for you?*

Teri: That makes me happy. I think it's not just that he's going to go to college. It's that he has some direction. I think that Robert having a direction is one step toward that miracle.

Joel: *Okay. The miracle happens, it's the next day. What would Robert and Mom be doing or saying that would make you less worried?*

Teri: If Mom got up and said, "Oh, I'm going to go for a walk this morning." That would be good for her and it would be good for me to see that. The thing I worry about the most – I sometimes have trouble sleeping at night – is worrying that something is going to happen to her or to Robert. That's been the biggest cause of anxiety or stress.

Joel: *Mom's getting up and walking, how is that related?*

Teri: I feel that after my dad passed away, it was like you never think that it's going to happen to you. I know people that it has happened to. It takes away that sense of immortality. Now that I know that it really can happen, I would want her to be the healthiest she could be so that that doesn't happen to her. It's not just seeing her healthy; I would want her to be as happy as she can be.

Joel: *Besides taking a walk, what other clues would there be that would tell you she's happier?*

Teri: Stuff like going to lunch with her friends, or going dancing. If she didn't have to do the paperwork all the time.

Joel: *If the miracle happened, would there be something different about your relationship?*

Teri: I don't think so. I think our relationship is really good.

Joel: *What's good about it?*

Teri: We are home a lot together. Before Robert came home, it was just me and Mommy. We have a good relationship. I feel if I were upset, or angry, or anything about any aspect of my life, I could go to her whether it were school, or work, or friends. I'm lucky I have that – some people don't.

Joel: *Nice.* [To Sharon] *What does Teri do that's helpful to you?*

Sharon: Just being there makes me happy. She takes after her father in being a little chipper all the time. She's chipper, and she's enthusiastic, and she's smart. She's ambitious, and nice, and does nice things for her friends. She's very busy with school. She has a very nice boyfriend who has a nice family. They do a lot of nice things together too. I really like him. I realize she has her life, but we're still very close.

Joel: *What about Robert? What does he do that's helpful?*

Sharon: I think just him coming home, and talking together. There was a period of time he wasn't talking to me.

Joel: *That's changed.*

Sharon: Yeah, that's changed.

Joel: *How did that change?*

Robert: I guess when Dad died, we started talking.

Joel: *What was the impetus for that? What's the relationship between Dad dying and you and Mom talking more?*

Robert: I realized that she's the only parent I have left.

Joel: *What does Mom do that's helpful to you?*

Robert: She helps me organize myself in terms of going to school.

Joel: [To Robert] *This miracle we are talking about; what's your picture?*

Robert: I guess just seeing everyone out of their rut that's been around since Dad left. I remember Mom being sad after Dad left and that's when things began going south.

Joel: *So, if the miracle happened and, as a result, people were getting out of their rut, what would be the first clue for you?*

Robert: Mom would be going for a walk, reading a book for pleasure, anything like that.

Joel: [To Sharon] *What would be the clue that the miracle was happening to Robert?*

Sharon: I'm thinking.

Joel: *Good. Take your time – thinking is good.* [All laugh.]

Sharon: Actually. part of the miracle has already happened. Robert came home and wants to go back to college. We can talk a little

Chapter 8 The Other Woman: Solution Focus With a Bereaved Family

bit more than we used to. There was a time that we weren't polite and nice to each other, and that's changed already. I think that has helped me an awful lot. I know he wants to work in the [New York] City. If the miracle happened, he would decide to stay and work here so we can get ourselves squared away. Maybe we can do some nice things. When he was 13 or 14, we used to take the dogs to the schoolyard for a walk. We haven't done that in such a long time. Robert said to me, "Let's take the dogs to the schoolyard for a walk." We did take the dogs; we're trying – the two of us are trying to do some nice things.

Joel: *You said pieces of the miracle are already happening.*
Sharon: Yes.
Joel: *In terms of moving you in the right direction, which ones have been the most helpful?*
Sharon: Having the two children. Especially having Robert home – that's been the biggest change. That has made a tremendous difference for me. There's still a lot of paperwork with the estate but I'm getting through that. We finally got Frank's mom on Medicaid and we're selling her house. I'm going up for tenure and that will be resolved soon. So, there are a lot of things happening that are positive; I just don't feel positive inside yet.
Joel: *What would need to happen for your insides to catch up with your outsides?*
Teri: It's being done, right?
Sharon: Yeah, just to have it off my shoulders. Maybe, then, I could move on with new stuff.
Joel: *Which is?*
Sharon: Happy stuff: dancing, meeting my friends for lunch. I have some very nice friends and I never see them. They call me up and ask me out and I say, "I don't feel good."
Joel: *How would your friends know about this miracle?*
Sharon: I might even call them. [Teri laughs.]

Discussion: The previous section is an example of how the Miracle Question serves to co-construct a solution focused conversation. Once I had a hint of the vision of change, I asked the Miracle Question. Not only did it develop the details of change and how the change will make a difference, but also the tenor of the conversation moved from problem to solution talk. There was a transformation from future to present exceptions. It is clear from the conversation that there is much that has happened already that has moved the family together in a positive direction.

Many of the questions are not only about the changes they personally will experience, but how they would notice that the changes are happening to each other. Teri and Robert's major concern is their mother. I accept this and pursue a conversation about how they would notice that the mother is happier. Then, with the presumption that Sharon is happier, how that would make a difference for them in their lives. The picture of change is expanded from Sharon to the rest of the family. This is an example of how solution focused practitioners view the individual as part of social systems, and that social systems are both the context and agent for positive change (de Shazer, 1991).

Joel: *So, the sense that I have from all of you is that pieces of this miracle are already happening. Do this for me. If I had a scale zero to ten, where ten is the miracle and zero is the total opposite of that, however you define that. Where would you put things right now?*

Robert: Three.

Teri: [Laughing] I was going to say "seven."

Joel: *He can say "three," you can say "seven" – that's fine.*

Sharon: I'm going to say "five."

Joel: *Five. Mom's going to split the difference. How's three different than zero?*

Robert: In the past month that I've been home, my relationship with Mom has improved. We're talking more, and we're going out to walk the dogs, and we went out to dinner the other day as a family – something we haven't done in a couple of years.

Joel: *Wow, really? Good reasons. Why seven?*

Teri: Since Robert's been home, I've seen a big improvement for me. Since he's been home there have been some changes. Since he's been home, he's been doing better, and taking steps in the right direction. So, from where he was a month ago to now is really a seven. When he was in Australia, I didn't talk to him for a good two months, at least. Now I see him every day, I see what he's doing, and he's going on his bike, and stuff like that. The way he acts towards me and towards Mom has changed tremendously.

Joel: [To Robert] *Did you realize the kind of impact you've had on your sister?*

Robert: I would hope so, yes.

Joel: *Is this a surprise, or something you pretty much knew?*

Chapter 8 The Other Woman: Solution Focus With a Bereaved Family

Robert: I knew about it.

Joel: *Mom, you said five; how's that different from zero? It's almost over the hump.*

Sharon: Yes, it's almost over the hump. Well, all these things are improving, as far as these legal things, and paperwork, and things like that. It's probably taking longer than it should because I'm not on top of it. I'm working on it. Of course, having Robert home is a major coup – accomplishment. He's anxious to go back to school, and has signed up for classes. All we have to figure out is how to pay for it. [All laugh.]

Robert: And where I'm going to live.

Sharon: Right. I want him to live on campus; they have nice dorms and good food. Teri has already had me out of zero. If it weren't for Teri, I would have been at zero.

Joel: *So, let's suppose things went one step higher. How would you know?*

Sharon: For me, it would be that we would do something together, like going to the City. We could go to a play. I would like to see us just a little bit more connected.

Joel: *That sounds important to you. What would it mean if you did that?*

Sharon: It would show that despite what's happened, we can still be a family. Terrible, terrible things have happened, but it would show that it's something that we can recover from. You never forget things that have happened. To tell you the truth, this [coming together to see a counselor] is a step in that direction.

Joel: *In what way?*

Sharon: If I had suggested it a year ago, Robert would have probably said, "What, are you crazy?" He wouldn't have come. For the past about two years, no one was ready to come. Maybe now we are ready to let each other know the certain feelings we have, and why we're acting this way. That's a great step – for us to be able to say things to one another. Not to hold it inside, and not understand what's going on with the other person.

Joel: *Teri, what about you? How would you know things went from seven to eight?*

Teri: I was going to say something along the lines of what Mom said. Everybody realizing that what happened is terrible, and it's not something you're ever going to forget, or completely get over, but your life does go on, and you can feel happy now in the same way you felt happy three years ago. We can still do things as a family. We have one less person, but we can still do things in the same way. Just because he's not here doesn't mean that everything is destroyed. We're still a family. We can be closer now than ever before.

Joel: *What would be the smallest thing in that line that would move you up?*

Teri: Maybe for the family dynamic to be better. It has gotten better with Robert coming home. There were times before he went to Australia that I felt I was the mediator. I feel that dynamic is gone.

Joel: *When did that change?*

Teri: I don't want to associate all the changes with Robert coming home. I don't want him to feel that I'm only happy if he stays home. That's not true. His being home is so vastly different than last time.

Joel: *How has your role changed?*

Teri: It's just normal now.

Joel: *Great. Three to four?*

Robert: I guess just enjoying life more.

Joel: *How would you know that?*

Robert: I guess doing things that normal people do. I see the things that Teri does and they're really great; I'm really proud of her. She graduated school, she's going back to school to get into med school, and volunteers, works, and goes out with her friends, and her boyfriend. I would want to do more stuff like that.

Joel: *For you, what would tell you that you were moving up that scale? Maybe one step – the normal stuff you'd be doing?*

Robert: For me personally?

Joel: *For both you and the family.*

Robert: Working and being productive; having friends I could go out with. We could do new, interesting, and exciting things.

Joel: *Like?*

Robert: Try different restaurants, or go to a museum, or go to the park, or go to a ball game.

Joel: *I want to ask one more of those scales and then take the break. It sounds like things are heading in the right direction. Each one of you said that pieces of the miracle have already started happening, even before you came here. Ten is you're really confident that this will continue, and probably even get better. Zero is this is just temporary. It's an illusion. Things are really worse than you think. Where would you put things on that scale?*

Sharon: I feel an eight. I'm feeling really good.

Chapter 8 The Other Woman: Solution Focus With a Bereaved Family

Teri: I was going to say seven or eight. I think we've been down at that really low point. There was a period of six months when I thought, "What else could happen to be worse than what's happened already? Will our house burn down? What else could happen?" We're just getting through that. We're all okay, and we're living here together a year and a half later. We've progressed little by little, and although it's taken this much time, I don't think there has been much regression.

Joel: Good.

Robert: For myself, personally, I would say probably seven or eight – in the right direction. As a family, I would put it lower though. Maybe five or six.

Joel: *Five or six – still pretty high. Why seven or eight?*

Robert: I'm really excited about going back to school. In the past year, I've learned a lot about what makes me happy. I can't really rely on other people to make me happy; it has to come from myself. I know I'll enjoy going to classes and learning. I'll work on the weekends for a company that I like. I'm excited about finishing that degree that will give me opportunities to do bigger and better things.

Joel: *Five or six is still pretty good, how come?*

Robert: It worries me that things will stay stagnant here when I go back to school. Mom has been sad for a really long time.

Joel: *What have you heard Mom say today that might mitigate that?*

Robert: I'm not sure. I think Mom has the steepest hill to climb because she took the divorce the worst of all of us by far – which is understandable. That was the catalyst, I think, for all of the problems. I think Dad's leaving was worse than his dying. His dying would be easier than feeling rejected. Until she resolves that, I'm not sure that she could truly be happy.

Joel: *So, how much of a surprise is it for you to hear her put herself at a five on that miracle scale, and an eight on the confidence scale?*

Robert: I think it's good, and we're all working towards getting better. It's still an up-hill battle. I've seen it affecting her for four years. It has gotten slightly better, but it's been four years and it's been tough. I would really like it to get better.

Joel: *What would need to happen, as far as the family is concerned, that would convince you that things could go higher?*

Robert: I think having everyone look back and be able to say, "There were good times, and the vast majority of times were good times." [To Mom] You know what I mean?

Sharon: Yes.

Joel: You do know what that means. [Sharon nods.] *I want to take that break. Is there anything else I should know, or anything particularly you want me to think about?*

Sharon: I don't think so.

Discussion: Robert's reaction to the conversation at the end of this section may be indicative of his experiencing a discordant pace. My reaction is to go more slowly and actually ask him to convince me (and therefore himself) that things could go higher on the scale.

Joel: [After the break] *Someone once said that life's one damn thing after another and you [Sharon] prove it. It's one thing that you lose somebody – twice – but then it's all the legal stuff. The paperwork, as you said, that drags on that serves to keep reminding you.*

Sharon: Yes.

Joel: *It makes sense that things are still up in the air. As you said, there are things that you'll never resolve. Despite that, I'm impressed with the hard work you've all been putting in. More importantly, it seems to be paying off. The one thing I've learned is that smart people come to useful realizations as a result of hard times. If you have to go through them, you may as well learn something useful from them. What you've all said is that as a result of this, you've come to realize how important family is. Teri said that we're mortal. Life is finite. I think for you, Robert, it pushed you in[to] making some decisions you need to go in life.*

Robert: Yeah.

Joel: *It's clearer to me just sitting here that the events of the past have brought you closer as a family. And the realization of how important that is. You've created a mutual support system together. Mom, you have some clear ideas about what would help move you up: dancing, going to the City with your kids, calling up friends and going out to dinner with them, going out walking, quitting smoking.*

Teri: [Laughs] I think that's something I want. I think that would make me happy.

Joel: *You can't forget those things that happen. What happens, at least in my experience, is that you begin to put it into perspective. That's the most useful thing. It sounds like some of that is happening. Something you said, Robert, is that you're responsible for your own happiness. You're right, and there's a component of happiness that's social. It's hard to sit at home doing nothing and being happy.*

Robert: Right.

Joel: *It's a lot easier to be out with friends and to be with family. I learned that there are three rules of life: if it isn't broken, don't fix it; if it works, do more of it; and if it isn't working, stop and do something that will. It sounds to me that what you are doing is working. So, I'm reluctant to fix what isn't broken, and want to keep pushing you in the right direction. I have a small suggestion. Each one of you might want to spend some time noticing the small pieces of the miracle happening day to day. I think it might be the most useful thing. I'll leave it up to you. Do you think it would be useful to come back and see me again – tell me what you're noticing?*

Sharon: [To Teri and Robert] What do you think?

Robert: I guess we'll play it by ear. Maybe a week or two – see how we're feeling.

Joel: *Okay. If you want to give me a call, we'll set up another appointment. Sounds good to me. If you don't call, good luck. I think you're heading in the right directions. Thanks for coming and letting me work with you.*

Sharon: I think it was really helpful to hear…we really never sat down too much. I'm sure I know how Robert feels, but not totally. I just got a little more insight into their thoughts and feelings, so I can work that way. You have to remember that we nurses like to help other people – that's what makes us happy! I now know more of what I can do to help. I can't thank you enough.

Discussion: This case example clearly demonstrates the difference between problem-solving and solution-building language-games. It also shows how the various solution-building tools combine to facilitate and maintain a solution-building conversation. Traditional practitioners might view working with families as more complicated than individual counseling. In reality, focusing on the individual without considering his or her social context is like trying to make meaning of a word outside of its sentence.

In fact, working with families is working with the social system. Both problems and solutions happen within people's life contexts. I enjoy working with families because the more people I have in the room, the richer the solution picture, and the greater the number of possibilities. Finally, the more people I have in the room, the more chance there is one who will be a strong customer for change.

"Change occurs because all individuals within a system affect and are affected by others. By its nature, SFBT is a systemic approach because it understands that significant and enduring change is as a result of small changes that affect clients and others in clients' lives. These small changes multiply and lead, ultimately, to larger changes" (de Shazer, 2007).

9 Changing Perspectives: Solution Focus With a Bereaved Client

> Give sorrow words: the grief that does not speak
> Whispers the o'er-fraught heart and bids it break.
> —*William Shakespeare,*
> **MacBeth,** *Act IV, Scene 3*

SESSION ONE

Martha's mother died one year prior to her request for bereavement counseling.

Joel: *What I usually do is somewhere along the line I'm going to take a break and that's usually when I run out of questions.*
Martha: Okay.
Joel: *Which takes me a long time because I get very curious. And I'm going to kind of review my notes and think about our conversation – write some ideas down, maybe a suggestion, something to think about, or try, or experiment – I don't know; we'll see what's appropriate and I'm going to come back and share that with you.*
Martha: Yeah, all right.
Joel: *So, it's your mom that died. When did she die?*
Martha: September 4th.

Joel: Of?
Martha: 2006.
Joel: What do you do?
Martha: I'm a school nurse/teacher.
Joel: So, you're a nurse/teacher. So you have two functions; is that what I gather? Or are you teaching nursing?
Martha: No, I have two functions, but for the most part I don't go into the classroom because it's covered with health education.
Joel: So, is that what you usually teach, health education?
Martha: [Nod's head.]
Joel: So, when you're not nurse/teaching, what do you do?
Martha: Well, I'm a wife.
Joel: So, you have a husband at home.
Martha: Yes, I do.
Joel: You're in possession of one of those. What's his name?
Martha: Tom.
Joel: Tom. Any kids?
Martha: Two; they're both older, and married, and out-of-state.
Joel: You've been successful as a parent. Hobbies, interests, things you enjoy doing?
Martha: I love sports. I love...
Joel: Watching, doing?
Martha: Doing.
Joel: Okay, what sports?
Martha: I love tennis, I love swimming, I love to watch baseball. I can't really participate in that, but I love to watch it. I like pretty much everything: hiking, biking. I like to do all those things.
Joel: And Tom shares that with you?
Martha: Oh, yeah.
Joel: Sounds like you guys have a good relationship.
Martha: Right. We have a disagreement about tennis versus racquetball.
Joel: Well, if that's the worst of your disagreements, you're doing pretty well. So your husband's at home and you have two kids out of the home. Anybody else?
Martha: That's pretty much it.
Joel: Friends?
Martha: Yeah, friends in the area: teachers, colleagues, things like that.
Joel: Great. That gives me the picture. So, well, I asked you a question on the phone and asked you to kind of suppose that our talk is going to be helpful to you. No sense doing it unless it's going to be.

Chapter 9 Changing Perspectives: Solution Focus With a Bereaved Client

Martha: Right.

Joel: *And so I wanted you to think about how you would know that it was being useful to you. Maybe after you leave today, maybe tomorrow, maybe a week or two weeks – whatever. So how would you know?*

Discussion: The prior conversation is meant to serve two purposes. First (the obvious), it begins the process of setting the direction of the conversation: Her information is important, and she is the expert on herself. The second is that the conversation is about a useful direction that will take place in her life outside of my office.

Martha: Well, the first thing I think I would ask is to stop crying as much as I cry.
Joel: *Okay, not crying as much as you cry.*
Martha: Right, and the second thing would be getting rid of the knot [in my stomach] and the nausea feeling I have a lot.
Joel: *Okay. So get rid of the knot. And what would be there instead.*

Discussion: Recall that one of the elements of a useful goal is the presence (rather than absence) of a difference. It is very usual for the client to begin direction formulation with a statement about what they do not want. My response is to ask her what would be happening instead of the negative.

Martha: Peace, peaceful feeling.
Joel: *Okay, right. And... what would Tom say if he were here and I asked him that same question about you? What would he say?*
Martha: He would agree. He would want to help me get through this process. And I really thought I could do it on my own and I really thought that at this point I should be better than I am.
Joel: *Okay, um.*
Martha: But I think it's worse. As time goes on, I don't feel like I get better, I feel like I get worse. You know, I thought I need[ed] time.
Joel: *Right, right. You said so he would notice that you would be getting through this process.*
Martha: Grieving process.
Joel: *Right, and what would tell him... what would be the first thing that would tell him that you would be getting through this process?*

Discussion: Clients often initially express the difference in emotional terms. Wittgenstein (1958) stated "internal process stands in need of external criteria" (p. 153) (see Chapter 3). The intent of this conversation is to help Martha describe the difference in behavioral terms. The easiest way to do this is to ask her to describe the difference from the viewpoint of someone else.

Martha: I suppose we could have conversations about my mom, and me not burst into tears. That I could go through her things, and not cry the whole time I was touching things. And that I could part with things that really shouldn't be there, you know what I'm saying?
Joel: *Right.*
Martha: Not think that I'm giving her away.
Joel: *Not thinking that you're giving her away.*
Martha: Or what I have of her.
Joel: *Um, huh, so, are there certain things that you would be keeping that would be kind of reminders?*
Martha: Um.
Joel: *Yeah? Like what?*

Discussion: This is reminiscent of Erickson's concept that problems are really failed solutions. Solutions that had served a purpose at one point but have long since lived out their usefulness. My assumption is that Martha has a good reason for wanting to keep some reminders of her mother, and I am being cautious about her throwing out the metaphorical baby with the metaphorical bath water.

Martha: I have her hairbrush with her hair in it in my dresser drawer. She was very eccentric in the little things that she kept – little trinkets. So I would probably keep some of those. But part with her clothes, things like that. Things someone else could really use. I can't seem to let go or...
Joel: *Let me ask... so what else would be different?*
Martha: Basically, I would find peace in knowing that she is better off. She was suffering, she wasn't having the quality of life that she would have liked to have continued, you know?
Joel: *Let me expand a little bit on... because it's going to help me kind of get a picture as detailed as possible of this picture of you getting through this process. And I have a strange question that I want to ask you that helps me do that?*

Chapter 9 Changing Perspectives: Solution Focus With a Bereaved Client

Martha: Okay.
Joel: But it's a strange question. Takes a bit of an imagination.
Martha: Okay.

Discussion: As soon as Martha stated that her husband would know that she was getting through the "grieving process," I realized that this was a perfect phrase to be used in the Miracle Question.

Joel: Let's suppose that after we talk today, you're going to leave here and go back and do what you normally do. I suppose you're going to go back to school today – do some work, get home, you and Tom will probably have dinner together, maybe.
Martha: Right.
Joel: Do what you do in the evening: watch TV, clean up, and you'll go to sleep tonight. Right?
Martha: Right.
Joel: And let's suppose that while you're sleeping, some miracle happens. And because of this miracle, you're getting through this process. [Snaps fingers.] *Just like that.*
Martha: That would be great.
Joel: Right, but you can't know about it – not yet, because it happened over the time you were sleeping. And the only way you can know about it is the small clues tomorrow when you wake up after this miracle happens. So that's my question. What would be the small clues for you that would tell you that this miracle happened? "I'm getting through this process."
Martha: I suppose it would be if I went into the room where I have her things stored at the moment that I would be able to put my hands on them and not cry.
Joel: Put your hands on the stuff and actually not cry.
Martha: Right. Um, I would...if she popped into my head, it wouldn't be – it wouldn't bring tears to my eyes. You know, because she pops into my head all day long. You know? I think those would probably...if I opened my dresser drawers and saw her hairbrush there that I would smile instead of cry.
Joel: Okay, okay. Right. So, I would suppose each one of those would have something to do with your thinking differently.
Martha: Um. [Nods head.]
Joel: I suppose because those kind of go together. So what would you notice about your thinking that would tell you that this miracle

happened? What would be the clues? How... when you walked into the room or when she popped into your head, what would you be thinking?*

Martha: That she wouldn't want me to feel this way.

Joel: *Okay.*

Martha: That she wouldn't want me to feel this way. That she wouldn't want me to feel I lost a part of myself.

Joel: *Okay.*

Martha: That she's looking down and smiling at me. Not wanting this for me.

Joel: *Okay. And what would she be wanting for you? How would she want you to be thinking, how would she want you to be feeling?*

Martha: She would want me to be happy. We had good times together, and she still loves me, and she's there.

Joel: *Okay.*

Martha: And she's smiling down on me and she's probably not happy that I'm crying all the time.

Joel: *So, if you were thinking more about the good times you had together...*

Martha: Right.

Joel: *Your history with her.*

Martha: Right.

Joel: *And if you were thinking about her being up there smiling down on you, how would that make a difference for you?*

Martha: I don't know, I think I would feel more peaceful. I do think I would be more peaceful. I have had, well, very few moments of peace since, but I remember having a dream one night and, I don't dream often, and in the dream, we hugged and when I woke up from the dream, I felt peaceful. I got some peace from that.

Discussion: Ah! An exception; my direction next is to expand on the exception and how it made a difference for her, and then to co-construct other exceptions.

Joel: *Interesting!*

Martha: We hugged, and talked, and I don't even remember the conversation, but I know we were talking, and hugging, and I felt so good to be able to hug her again.

Joel: *Wow! Great.*

Martha: And another time I was... a dream I was driving and I had her things in the back of the car. And, this was shortly after she passed,

Chapter 9 Changing Perspectives: Solution Focus With a Bereaved Client

I said, "I need to know you're okay." I had cards she had gotten, and flower vases, and things like that in the back of the car. Stupid dream, but the flower stood up – you know just stood up – and I guess that was a sign to let me know she was okay.
Joel: *And that made a difference for you?*
Martha: That made a difference. A little bit, yeah.
Joel: *In what way?*
Martha: I have images of her being fine. I have images of her running as a little girl, running through fields of daisies, and my uncles are there, and she's really enjoying herself. And I think that's great, that's what I want, but...

Discussion: It is not unusual when doing bereavement work that clients report incidents that border on, or actually reflect, the supernatural. The issue is not whether such events are real; the question is how one utilizes such reports to help drive the solution-building process. Notice the conscious attempt here to interrupt Martha. The ending sentences start out "and I think that's great" and she begins to add the "but." This suggests to me that she is moving into problem talk and I want to continue her in solution building.

Joel: *These moments of peace, they only happen during the time you sleep or do you actually have these during... do you have these few moments...?*
Martha: No, I've never had any during the... well, my wake time.
Joel: *It's usually when you're sleeping, usually because of the dream.*
Martha: Right.
Joel: *Um.*
Martha: Well, when I woke up after those dreams, I felt more at peace, yeah.
Joel: *Great. How long did that last?*

Discussion: Language consists of the whole of the verbal and nonverbal. Even the simplest grunt can be co-constructed as meaningful. I gave Martha time to rethink her answer when I did not jump on her response that she never has moments of peace during the time she is awake, and instead responded (or nonresponded in this case) with a simple "um"...

Martha: For a while, maybe through half the morning.
Joel: *Excellent. Good.*

Martha: Yeah.
Joel: *Good. How did you kind of maintain that for that long? How were you able to keep that going?*
Martha: I don't know. Maybe taking about it.
Joel: *To?*
Martha: My husband.

Discussion: It is very easy to view dreams and their results as random events over which we have no control. The attempt here is to co-construct that. While she may not have control over her dreams, she does have control over how she makes meaning of them – which language-game she chooses to be in.

Joel: *And what did you say to him?*
Martha: I just told him what I dreamed, you know. I might have told my children too. And it might have made me feel a little more buoyant.
Joel: *Great. And when you did that, what did they do that kind of helped it continue?*
Martha: Well, my son said to me, because I was going through bouts of this at night and I told him about the first dream, and he said "Mom, don't you get it? That was a sign from grandma." He probably put it more in perspective than I even could, you know?
Joel: *That's great. So you haven't yet found, or seen these, or kind of noticed these moments of peace during your waking time?*

Discussion: The word "yet" is both small and very meaningful.

Martha: Basically, I try very, very hard to stay busy. So I don't have to think. And when I'm busy, I don't think, but as soon as I drive, or I sit down, or I do anything, then everything floods in. But as long as I can keep busy, and organize, and do my tasks I can avoid it.
Joel: *Right, because you're thinking about something different.*
Martha: Correct. Or I have someone else's problems that I'm dealing with and trying help them solve. You know what I'm saying?
Joel: *Right.*
Martha: And I don't have to face my own.
Joel: *Right, so you're still able to do your work, still able to…*
Martha: For the most part. For the most part, yeah. I think I'm still very, very effective. I sometimes wonder. I don't have the energy that I had, you know what I mean, so from that perspective I feel a little weaker.
Joel: *So again, if the miracle happened…*

Chapter 9 Changing Perspectives: Solution Focus With a Bereaved Client

Discussion: I re-anchored the miracle to move from problem back to solution talk.

Martha: I would have more energy.
Joel: Yeah. How would you notice that?
Martha: I guess I wouldn't be so tired all the time. I would feel like I could keep going. Because there are times when... I don't recall ever not feeling like I could keep going. I still have that little extra energy that I could tap into and use. I don't feel that anymore. When I get tired, I get tired. I just want to stop.
Joel: Right, right, okay. And you do – you keep going?
Martha: Well sometimes I don't have a choice.
Joel: So, how do you do it?
Martha: I just try to... maybe not as slowly, not as fast, not as...
Joel: Kind of conserve energy.
Martha: Right.
Joel: So, again, what would Tom notice at this miracle? How would he know it happened to you?
Martha: I don't know whether I said I don't cry, or not talking, or thinking, not tear up. I don't feel so heavy hearted. He would notice all of that. Because...
Joel: How would he notice it?
Martha: I would, I guess... I've always been a high-energy person.
Joel: So he would see some of the energy coming back?
Martha: Yeah, he would see that. He would also probably see that I was a little more cheerful. Because I've always been a very cheerful person. I don't usually let things bother me. And I just haven't been able to do that anymore.
Joel: What would be the smallest change that he would notice?
Martha: The smallest change. Oh, wow! I guess I wouldn't feel so overwhelmed when I was doing things at home.
Joel: So, how would he know that? What would he notice different about that?
Martha: I don't know, that I would be a little better with things I have to do at home. And not complain maybe.
Joel: Okay. And your colleagues at school, what would they notice different.
Martha: I don't think they'd notice anything different other than the fact that I, sometimes when the conversation turns to talking, I'll tear up a little bit, but I would stop that. That would be the only thing

they would notice. But for the most part, I manage to get through the school day without anyone being aware.

Joel: *When is there a time when you're working in school that you get something that's close to that peaceful feeling? May not be there, but close to it?*

Martha: During the school day, I keep myself so busy, I don't think about it. If I can keep myself busy and not have to deal with everything, I'm fine. And for the most part, like I said, I tend to be more of a high-energy person and I like to stay busy, and I do that. Sometimes my friends will stop, and they'll talk, and in the conversations, you know, I'll tear up like that.

Joel: *And so they would...*

Martha: They'll console me, yes, they console me.

Joel: *So, let's do this. If I had a scale of zero to ten, and ten is the miracle, and zero is the day your mother died. Where would you put things right now?*

Martha: Maybe on a two or three.

Joel: *Okay, wow! Two or three; how come?*

Martha: Well, you know what, I don't even know if I could say two or three. Because initially when she passed, of course I was very, very upset and sad but as time goes on, I mean, I was so busy trying to make arrangements and talk to people and do all those things I have to. But as time goes on, and I recognize how much I miss her every day, and it's worse, actually, instead of getting better, which is one of the reasons that I thought by now I'd be much farther along this process, you know? And I keep thinking, is there something wrong with me? Am I not getting the picture? I mean, am I not able to move on? Am I stuck in a rut somewhere, you know? So I'm not sure. So two or three is being optimistic.

Discussion: There are a couple of lessons here. One needs to be cautious about how enthusiastic the response is to a scaling number – especially those in the lower range of the scale. When the pace is incongruent to clients, it may give them pause so that they may believe that the response was too optimistic. They then feel obliged to lower their responses.

The other lesson I learned from Martha is something about a common response to bereavement. After this session with Martha, I began to pay special attention to clients' statements about their reactions to the death of a significant other. I found that it is very usual for clients to report, similar to Martha, that they were occupied for the first few weeks with the presence of friends, and family, and a general sense of "numbness." Once everyone leaves, and the death becomes real for them, they begin the grieving process. I have learned that it is usually useful to set zero at two or three weeks after the death.

Joel: *So, let's be optimistic. What puts you up at two or three?*
Martha: Because I know suddenly it's a reality maybe instead of a dream.
Joel: *Okay, that you've finally come to grips with the fact that she's gone.*
Martha: Correct. Something I'm dreaming, that it'll pass; you know? I do know in my heart that she's not suffering any more. So, that puts it maybe a two or three. That gives me some peace, some comfort.
Joel: *Where would Tom put you on that scale if he were here?*
Martha: I don't know where he would put me.
Joel: *What's your guess?*
Martha: My guess is that it makes him so sad that I'm so sad. And he would probably say a two or three.
Joel: *So he would put you about the same. And if I asked him how two or three is different from zero, what would he say?*
Martha: That I am able to be somewhat productive I guess.
Joel: *Right, what else?*
Martha: That there are...we can have good times together. That I can enjoy being with my grandchildren – I can have a sense of peace just being with them.
Joel: *You can?*
Martha: Yeah, while we're doing that, I put things out of mind, but as soon as I have...
Joel: *Some downtime.*

Discussion: There is a technique in Ericksonian trance work where the clinician states the negative before the client can think it. The previous transaction is an example of that use in normal conversation. When I put the words to her experience, I am essentially preempting problem talk.

Martha: Correct.
Joel: *Martha, You've given me a lot to think about. So, I want to take that break. But before I do, is there anything else that you think I should know that would be helpful, or is there anything, particularly, that you want me to think about?*

Martha: The only thing I can think of is I don't think anybody realizes how much we struggled.

Joel: *You and Mom?*

Martha: Yeah. I'm talking about things that people in today's world can't even imagine.

[Martha explained how she and her mother lived without running water, electricity, and other conveniences that most people take for granted. She also described how her mother was not educated, and struggled in life.]

Joel: [After the break] *Martha, what I've learned from working with people here is that there is no time frame for these things: Some people take shorter to heal, some people take longer. I've also learned that it's never in a straight line. Sometimes you have to take one step back in order to take two steps forward. But I can understand your impatience. You want to get through this.*

Your mom sounds like she was a remarkable woman. She wasn't educated, but she sure knew what mattered. And you were close to Mom; you went through a lot together. She didn't give up. So I think that kind of optimism – you inherited that. Because my sense of it is that she kept plugging because she felt just around the corner things will be better. And I can understand why she was proud of you. As I said, you inherited a lot from Mom: I think your commitment, your sense of pride, knowing what counts, and – the sense I have – your optimism. I can see that's part of what Mom left you, also – her legacy.

My sense of you is kind of – how do I put this – that it's like you're on the verge. I get the sense that you're on the verge. There are some things right now that tell me that.

You can enjoy life: you do your hiking, your biking, your swimming. You remain optimistic – after all, that's why you're here. If you didn't think things could be better, you wouldn't be sitting in that chair. You can kind of envision the difference. You know how you want to be thinking, and doing, and feeling better, what would make a difference, that you have a nice network of friends, colleagues, and family that encourage you. And there are these moments of peace that you have.

Martha: I wish they would happen more often.

Joel: *Well...*

Martha: I want to hug her at night more often.

Chapter 9 Changing Perspectives: Solution Focus With a Bereaved Client

Joel: I know. Interesting, because when you said... does it happen during the day, you said "no" and then you remembered a time that it was when you were with your grandchildren. So they do happen. You talked about Mom guiding the family. Well, she's doing that through you.

You talked about getting through the grieving process. It's interesting to me that many people have this idea that there's this process that takes place: you grieve and then you go on with life. So it's either you're grieving, or you're going on with life. To me, the more I work here, the more I realize that it's "both/and." Both grieving and moving on are happening at the same time. People get so focused on one that they miss the other. In some ways, this is a problem of perspective – of viewing.

I have a small suggestion that might be helpful. I don't know, we'll see. But I would suggest that you spend the next couple of weeks really taking a hard look at those small, brief times of peace. I'm not interested in quantity right now. I'm interested in quality. So it doesn't matter to me if it happens a minute a day. It matters that you notice it. That make sense?

Martha: Yes.

Joel: You might even want to think back, and write those things down at the end of the day so you can actually see them happening. You might even want to enlist your husband in watching for those, too. Sometimes he may be more aware of it, watching you, than you.

Martha: That's possible, yeah. It's questions I never asked him.

Joel: Might be a useful thing for you to do. See what he finds. It's not the answer, it's a start. We'll see where it goes.

Martha: That's what I want to do. I want to start, yeah.

Joel: So, I guess the first question is, do you think it will be helpful to make another time to sit down and talk?

[Martha chose to return and we set two weeks for the next visit.]

Discussion: There are messages here that I have found over time to be common, and useful with a large majority of bereavement clients.

- Time frame: Many people have sought me out because they believe, or they have been told by others, that they should have healed already. It is useful for them to hear an "expert" tell them to take their time, and that "normal" covers a lot of territory.

- Process: I recall once receiving a call from someone who wanted to talk to an expert on the grieving process. He told me that a friend of his suggested that he should inquire about the 21 steps of healing. I have found that another useful message is that each person has a unique way of healing and there are no steps in the process. This alleviates clients from thinking that there is a right way and a wrong way to heal. The major question is simply, "What are they doing that makes a difference?"
- She is Mom's legacy: it is often useful to list the ways in which the client has integrated characteristics of the bereaved. The implication here is that the significant other continues to live through them – the client is the legacy.
- "Either/or" versus "both/and": Grieving is not separate from life; it is part of it. Grieving is not a separate process from healing – they coexist. The conversation can be helpful when it co-constructs the healing that is taking place at the same time as the grieving.

SESSION TWO: E.A.R.S.

Berg (1994) describes the process of re-establishing and maintaining the solution-building process after the first session. She lists four components with the acronym of E.A.R.S.: Elicit, Amplify, Reinforce, and Start again.

Elicit

What's Better?: This is how the clinician elicits how the client made things even a little bit better on his own. (Berg, 1994, p. 150)

There is an assumption that something happened between sessions that is better and useful to the client. The clinician's job is to elicit the difference. The simplest way to do this is to start the question with the question, "What's better since we last met?" There are three possible responses to this: 1) something is, indeed, better; 2) nothing is better; and 3) things are, in fact, worse.

Something Is Better: This is certainly the easiest one of the three to co-construct. If the client reports that something happened that made a positive difference for them, the clinician can proceed directly to amplification.

Nothing Is Better: My immediate thought when the client responds with "nothing is better" is "something has to be better, and the client missed it." The most useful response in this case is asking the client to describe each day and what happened. Inevitably, the client will describe even the smallest difference. This requires the clinician to listen carefully with "solution ears."

Things Are Worse: My experience is that this is actually easier to deal with than the "nothing is better" response. What I have found in the majority of cases is that something had happened that day, or the previous day prior to the client's appointment, that has colored the perception of the whole week. When the client reports the problem (which often they do), the clinician can then ask what was better during the period prior to the incident. The other useful response is to ask the client which day or days were the best and then follow with amplification.

I recall one therapist responded to "things are worse" by asking the client which day was the best, and then co-constructing the details of what was better that day. Once the client went through the process, she mused how she allowed an argument that day with her husband to color her whole week.

Scaling is another alternative for eliciting the difference. When I was supervising a community mental health clinic, the staff and I wondered whether scaling would be affected by when it was asked. We knew that there was a greater tendency in the first session for the client to scale him- or herself higher after the miracle question than before. We were curious whether this would hold true in the second session and beyond.

We devised an experiment whereby we would randomly assign 50 second-session clients to one of two different groups via a coin toss. Group one was asked "What's better?" followed by a scale later in the session per usual practice; group two was asked a progress scale immediately. We were essentially interested if there were any significant difference in where clients scaled themselves depending upon the group they were assigned.

What we found, in fact, was that clients tended to place themselves at about the same place no matter whether the scale was asked in the beginning or at the end of the session. There are some advantages with beginning a session around a scale. The major one is that it avoids the no change/worse responses and therefore simplifies the E.A.R.S. process.

Amplify

Once a change is elicited, the next step is to co-construct it as a change that makes a difference. The next series of questions are about the details of what was different, how it made a difference to the client, who else noticed it, what difference did it make to others in the client's life, and what would be the likely results if it continued.

Reinforce

Berg (op. cit.) describes this next step:

> There are many subtle and not so subtle ways to reinforce any positive changes the client is making. Raising an eyebrow, a surprised look, confusion about what you heard, and so on, are all nonverbal ways to reinforce this as something different. "Wow" is a wonderful way to say a lot without saying a great deal. "What did you say you did?" while leaning forward with an incredulous look on your face will highlight the changes and reinforce the good decision the client made. Other reinforcing questions are: "Not everyone (your age, in your situation, with your problem, etc.) can do that. So, are you the kind of person who 'just does things because it is the right thing to do?' I wonder where you learned that? Was it hard to do, I mean getting up on time? How did you force yourself to get up?" (p. 152)

Start Again: Once the process has been completed, and the clinician has elicited, amplified, and reinforced the difference, the clinician can begin the process over by simply asking, "What else?" Once there have been several co-constructions of "better," the client can be asked a scaling question (or several) before the clinician takes the break, and returns with complements.

Martha's second session is a good example of E.A.R.S. in action.

Joel: *What's been better since last I saw you – even just a little bit?*
Martha: A lot. Like you said, I really did have peaks and valleys. I went through a very, very stressful time and that made it more difficult to deal with. So, I'm not as emotional as I was.
Joel: *Good, okay.*
Martha: I did visit my grandchildren and that was great.
Joel: *You said that was something that gives you some sense of peace.*
Martha: Right. I got a call when I got there that my cousin passed away – he was very young. So, as sad as that was, I got some sense of peace

Chapter 9   Changing Perspectives: Solution Focus With a Bereaved Client   173

from that, knowing that my mom was there to welcome, and embrace her. Also, having family around who knew what I was going through was good.

Joel: *You said that things were not quite as emotional. What did you mean?*

Martha: I still tear easily, but not as easily as I did before. I think just before we met last time, it was her birthday and that was tough. I expect I'm going to have a difficult time because the anniversary of her death is coming up.

Joel: *Okay. So, what would be helpful?*

Martha: To prevent it?

Joel: *Well, prevent might be too strong a word. I guess...what will be helpful for you to get through it?*

Martha: My mental outlook could be more positive.

Joel: *Mental outlook?*

Martha: I guess realizing that she is at peace.

Joel: *Realizing she's at peace. How close are you to that?*

Martha: I guess I'm closer, but those other times when I'm worn down and stressed, it's harder for me to accept.

Joel: *Less energy.*

Martha: Less energy, yes.

Joel: *And those other times when you have more energy?*

Martha: I'm able to put things in better perspective.

Discussion: Here is an example of "listening with solution ears." She states that sometimes she has less energy, which implies that there are times she does.

Joel: *And what's "a better perspective?"*

Martha: She did have a very good life, and she did live longer than any of us had expected or anticipated. We didn't have to make these terrible decisions about life support or those sorts of things.

Joel: *Um. Very often what I hear is that the anticipation is worse than the actual event.*

Martha: Right.

Joel: *What would be the clue that this was true for you?*

Martha: I guess the first thing would be that I wouldn't tear up as much.

Joel: *You said that that's already happened to some extent.*

Martha: To some extent, yeah. That I could have a conversation with relatives or friends and not break up.

Joel: *Oh, and how much of that is happening now?*
Martha: A friend can ask me about Mom and sometimes I don't break up.
Joel: *Any idea what makes the difference?*
Martha: No, no idea.
Joel: *Is it the individual, for example, your husband?*
Martha: No, not all the time with my husband.
Joel: *So, it's not the individual.*
Martha: No, it's not the individual. Gosh, I don't know!

Discussion: While the previous segment may seem to reflect problem solving, that was not the intent. The purpose of this conversation was to deconstruct the frame that her "breaking up" is a constant. Her last statement ("Gosh, I don't know!") may be an indication that she became curious about those exceptions. In and of itself, it suggests that she has accepted that exceptions happen, and therefore exceptions are possible.

Joel: *So besides tearing up, what else might Tom notice different?*
Martha: I think he thinks that I'm not making progress fast enough. He would want me to move faster.
Joel: *So, your sense is that you're moving forward faster than he's recognizing.*
Martha: Correct.

Discussion: Harry Korman (personal communication) calls this type of intervention a "therapeutic misunderstanding." She said that Tom might think that she's not making progress as fast as she should. I suggested that maybe she is moving faster than he recognizes. She has the option of correcting my misunderstanding, but instead accepts that she is moving faster than he is aware.

Joel: *How would he know that the internal is becoming more external for him?*
Martha: I think, perhaps, if I didn't refer to her as often.
Joel: *Okay, and what would you be talking about instead?*
Martha: Maybe day-to-day activities, or planning events for the two of us.
Joel: *Great.*
Martha: We're trying to do that.
Joel: *You are?* [Leans forward.] *What do you mean?*
Martha: Just that we don't stay in a rut, and stay home rather than going out.
Joel: *Where have you been going?*
Martha: We went to Cold Spring [New York] and walked around, and we went to a ballgame. So we've done some things.

Joel: *So, planning more of those would be the sign for him?*
Martha: And not referring to Mom so much.
Joel: *Planning the events that you have – Cold Spring, ballgames – how has that made a difference for you?*
Martha: I enjoy being out, and I'm a social creature, and I love people. I try not to think about it, but sometimes I regress and something happens that reminds me.
Joel: *Of course. Of course you do. How is talking about your mother helpful to you?*

Discussion: Much has been written on the role of relationship and empathy in therapy. There's no doubt that both are important and account for about a third of successful clinical outcomes (Miller et al., 1997).

Empathy is a sine qua non of therapy. If the client does not perceive that the therapist is sincerely empathetic, there can be no therapeutic relationship. Dolan and Nelson (2007) state:

> Empathy is very important in this work and such statements tell the client that you understand, help with pacing, and help the client prepare for solution building. Empathic statements help to set up a "yes and" rather than "yes, but" tone. (p. 254)

The question then arises: What constitutes an empathic response? This can be reflected in the simplest ways: a shake of the head, a brief exclamation, a grunt, or just a simple, "Of course." No more may be needed to convey to the client that the therapist can share a common human experience.

Martha: Well, my family reminds me that it was her time, and I guess that's helpful, but I try not to think about it. I try to deny it and keep going and try not to think about the past. At the point where it's not a constant impression, I think I'll feel more peaceful.
Joel: *You must have a good reason to talk to Tom about your mom.*

Discussion: This is an example of helping the client deconstruct the problem and re-construct it as a solution. It is also an example of how solution focused therapists "blame" the client for having a brain.

Martha: Well, she lived with us for many years, and he misses her too. He was surprised that she lived as long as she did, and that I should count my blessings that I had as much time with her as I did.

Joel: *It sounds like you do!*
Martha: Yes, I do.
Joel: *Those are not contradictory – the regret and the joy.*
Martha: That's true.
Joel: *So, let me do one of those scales with you.*
Martha: Sure.
Joel: *Let's say that ten is, in terms of what you were hoping our conversation would do for you, ten is right there. Zero is the total opposite. Where would you put things?*

Discussion: Scales, such as this one, are useful in helping to keep therapy brief.

Martha: I would put it at seven or eight because it has helped. It helped put things in better perspective because I can now recognize all the benefits rather than all the negatives.
Joel: *Great. Is seven or eight at this point good enough?*
Martha: Well, it's getting me through a little bit easier. I'm not as exhausted. I have more energy. That has helped my mind set too. I'm reflecting more on what my mom would want, and she wouldn't want me to be this way.
Joel: *So, that thought has come more to the fore? [She nods.] And that thought is more helpful to you?*
Martha: Yes.
Joel: *So could things get higher than seven or eight, do you think?*
Martha: I think they could. I need to remember her good advice and that will keep me on the straight and narrow.
Joel: *How would you know that things went from seven or eight, to eight or nine?*
Martha: I would smile more when I think about her advice.
Joel: *When are there times that you can smile more when you think about her advice?*
Martha: There are, there are. I can think about her idiosyncrasies and laugh about it. I know I'm going to get there, but getting there is such a struggle right now.
Joel: *Right. How confident are you ... if I had another of those scales where ten is that you're really confident that you can stay at least around that seven or eight, and zero is a total lack of confidence, where would you put yourself?*

Chapter 9 Changing Perspectives: Solution Focus With a Bereaved Client

Discussion: My decision to ask this scale was based upon the principle of making sure I go more slowly than she is willing to go.

Martha: Well, I know I'll have a drop on the anniversary of her death. I'm not planning that; I want to celebrate her life.

Discussion: My immediate thought, as she said this was, her protestations aside, she is co-constructing the problem already when she states that she knows she will have a "drop" on the anniversary. I realized at this point that I need to help her deconstruct what will likely become a self-fulfilling prophesy, and help her co-construct possibilities rather than problems.

Joel: *How would celebrating her life make a difference for you on the anniversary?*
Martha: It would put it in perspective that she is where she needs to be, and I am where I need to be, and she would want me to move forward.
Joel: *Okay. What's the lowest on that scale you could imagine getting on the anniversary?*
Martha: Maybe a five or six.
Joel: *Wow! So what is it, do you think, that helps you not get lower than that five or six?*
Martha: Just knowing her, and knowing the things she would say to me.
Joel: *And what will it be after the anniversary that will get you back up?*
Martha: The day itself will be sad.
Joel: *Of course.*
Martha: Knowing that she had a really good life, loved, and was loved.
Joel: *So, what will surprise you on the anniversary?*
Martha: I suppose I would be surprised if I didn't feel sad – celebrate and not feel sad about her passing.
Joel: *"Celebrate" meaning?*
Martha: Celebrate that she had a wonderful life, and this is the anniversary of that.
Joel: *How would you celebrate that?*
Martha: In my thoughts, and in my prayers, I think.
Joel: *What are you learning from this experience?*
Martha: I'm learning to put my thoughts in a better light, and in a better frame – not center them so much on how much pain I'm feeling. I'm putting more thoughts on where she is, and being in peace instead of my loss.

Joel: Um, that's good, good. Well, I'm going to take a break. Anything you need to tell me?

Martha: I don't think so.

Joel: [After the break] *I'm really impressed with the hard work you've been doing. It really is hard work changing perspective. It's even harder to change the way you feel.*

Martha: It takes time.

Joel: *You're right; it does take time, and it also takes hard work, it requires a lot of energy. Not only are you changing perspective, but you also do some things that seem to be very useful to you, like planning special events with Tom, and doing more social things. It makes perfect sense to me that you would be doing that. You're right that peaks and valleys are part of the process. Sooner or later the peaks and valleys begin to even off – I guess you get the plains.* [Both laugh.] *It seems to be moving in that direction. Sadness and joy are not opposites. It makes sense that you're sad about losing her, and it also makes sense that you can be joyful about her life; how she has touched you, and how you have gained from her existence.*

What I'm also impressed with is that you seem to have some good ideas about what will be helpful on the anniversary. You could be sad that day. That doesn't mean it has to be a sad day – could be a joyful day. I thought about that, and came up with three suggestions. I'll let you decide which will be the most useful, or you can decide to do something yourself. First is seeing if you can guess, without asking him, what Tom might be noticing that will tell him that you're moving forward. The second is planning something for the anniversary that will help you change perspective. I don't know, maybe something like planting a tree in memory of your mother. The last one is sitting down each evening before the anniversary day, and writing down all those things that you would want to remember and celebrate on that day. Pick a certain time on that day and read what you wrote. Those are some suggestions I might have.

Martha: Okay.

Joel: *I'm thinking that you're well on your way, and you might not need me anymore. I don't want to throw you out…*

Martha: No, that's okay.

Joel: *I'm here if you need me, but it sounds like you made a good enough beginning to me.*

Martha: I appreciate your help.

Joel: *If you're inclined to give me a progress report, feel free.*

Martha: Okay, I will. I really appreciate it, I really do.

Afterword

EULOGY

I was in my sophomore year of college and had returned from the Thanksgiving recess. About a week after my return to campus, I came back to the dorm after classes and received a message that it was urgent that I call my brother-in-law, Sam. "Joel," he said, "Your dad is very sick and in the hospital. We have a plane ticket reserved for you at the airport. You need to come home tomorrow."

When I deplaned the next day in Rochester, my sister, Sandy, and my brother-in-law were there to greet me. Sandy hugged me, letting me know that Dad had died of a cerebral hemorrhage the previous night. The next few days were a blur to me: the funeral, the cemetery, the friends, relatives, and strangers coming and going in Sandy's house where we were sitting *Shiva*.

I was grateful to return back to college; I had my studies and activities to occupy me. My mother, however, was faced now with a life alone. While she had worked before marrying my father and sporadically after (mostly part-time during the busy holiday season in December), she was basically a stay-at-home mom raising three children, of whom I was the youngest.

My mother had never completed high school, something she had regretted in her adult life. She was determined that her children would graduate from college, for the lessons of her life taught her that education is to be held in high regard. She was successful on that account. All three of us graduated college, and two went on for advanced degrees. Now she was faced with a life alone, little job experience, and financial responsibilities.

My father was a blue-collar worker – a refrigeration repairman. We were not rich by any stretch of the imagination, and he did not leave very much in the way of financial resources for my mother after he died just short of his 61st birthday. Mom subsisted on Social Security survivor's benefits but the writing was clearly on the wall: she needed to find another source of income. In addition to this, she was living in housing meant for families. Not long after my father's death, she was informed, as apologetically as possible, that she would need to find another place to live.

My mother was a remarkable person: energetic, goal directed, and optimistic. She loved my father and missed him dearly, but she also realized that she needed to do something to get on with her life. She enrolled in the Manpower program and went everyday to take classes to prepare for her G.E.D. and to train as a secretary. One of the proudest moments of her life came when she earned her high school diploma.

Once she had completed the program, Mom obtained a job as a secretary with a local union. She found a one-bedroom apartment located in a nice section of the city, close to my sister. Eventually, she remarried – a long-time friend of the family, a widower who had lost his wife many years before. She lived a long life, surrounded by her children, grandchildren, and great grandchildren, and passed peacefully at 96.

I recall reminiscing with my brother after her funeral. He recalled that she had had a hard life, and I suppose that there is some truth in that. She had an indomitable spirit and a basic philosophy of life, "No excuses, just do it," long before Nike took on that motto. She believed that we set our own direction; that we are responsible for our lives, and, more importantly, we are responsible for how we make meaning of the events in our lives. The meaning of my father's death, therefore, was as much about life as it was about grief. If at this journey's end, there is somewhere that the righteous go, then my mom has earned her place.

My intention was not to write a book about death and grief; it was to write a book about life, hope, and celebration. Most of all, it is a book about how we make choices about usefully misunderstanding the events that happen to us. Death and loss are not problems to be solved – they are what give life its meaning.

> *I went to the dances at Chandlerville,*
> *And played snap-out at Winchester.*
> *One Time we changed partners,*
> *Driving home in the moonlight of middle June,*
> *And then I found Davis.*
> *We were married and lived together for seventy years,*
> *Enjoying, working, raising the twelve children,*
> *Eight of whom we lost*

Ere I had reached the age of sixty.
I spun, I wove, I kept the house, I nursed the sick,
I made the garden, and for holiday
Rambled over the fields where sang the larks,
And many a flower and medicinal weed –
Shouting to the wooded hills, singing to the green valleys.
At ninety-six I had lived enough, that is all,
And passed to a sweet repose.
What is this I hear of sorrow and weariness,
Anger, discontent and drooping hopes?
Degenerate sons and daughters,
Life is too strong for you –
It takes life to love life.

Edgar Lee Masters,
"Lucinda Matlock," *Spoon River Anthology*

References

Abate, F. (Ed.). (1997). *The Oxford desk dictionary and thesaurus*. New York: Oxford University Press.

Allumbaugh, D. L., & Hoyt, W. T. (1999). Effectiveness of grief therapy. A meta-analysis. *Journal of Counseling Psychology, 46*, 370–380.

Anderson, H., & Goolishian, H. (1992). The client is the expert: A not-knowing approach to therapy. In S. McNamee & K. J. Gergen (Eds.), *Therapy as social construction* (pp. 25–39). London: Sage.

Bateson, G. (1972). *Steps to an ecology of mind*. New York: Ballantine Books.

Bavelas, J. B., McGee, D., Phillips, B., & Routledge, R. (2000). Microanalysis of communication in psychotherapy. *Human Systems, 11*, 47–66.

Benton, R. (1978). *Death and dying: Principles and practices in patient care*. New York: D. Van Nostrand.

Berg, I. K. (1994). *Family based service: A solution focused approach*. New York: Norton.

Berg, I. K., & de Shazer, S. (1993). Making numbers talk. Language in therapy. In S. Friedman (Ed.), *The new language of change: Constructive collaborations in psychotherapy* (pp. 5–24). New York: Guilford Press.

Berg, I. K., & Miller, S. (1992). *Working with the problem drinker: A solution focused approach*. New York: Norton.

Bonanno, G. A. (2004). Loss, trauma, and human resilience: Have we underestimated the human capacity to thrive after extremely aversive events? *American Psychologist, 59*, 20–28.

Brill, A. A. (Ed.). (1938). *The basic writings of Sigmund Freud*. New York: Random House.

Byock, I. (1997). *Dying well: The prospect for growth at the end of life*. New York: Riverhead Books.

Cade, B. (2007). Springs, streams, and tributaries: A history of the brief solution focused approach. In T. Nelson & F. Thomas (Eds.), *Handbook of solution focused brief therapy: Clinical applications*. New York: Haworth.

Campbell, J., Elder, J., Gallagher, D., Simon, J., & Taylor, A. (1999). Crafting the tap on the shoulder: A compliment template for solution focused therapy. *The American Journal of Family Therapy, 27*(1), 35–47.

Cantwell, P., & Holmes, S. (1994). Social construction: A paradigm shift for system therapy & training. *Australia and New Zealand Journal for Family Therapy, 15*(1), 17–26.

De Jong, P., & Hopwood, L. E. (1996). Outcome research on treatment conducted at the Brief Family Therapy Center 1992–1993. In S. D. Miller, M. A. Hubble, & B. L. Duncan (Eds.), *Handbook of solution focused brief therapy* (pp. 272–298). San Francisco: Jossey-Bass.

de Shazer, S. (1982). *Patterns of brief family therapy*. New York: Guilford.

de Shazer, S. (1985). *Keys to solutions in brief therapy*. New York: Norton.
de Shazer, S. (1988). *Clues: Investigating solutions in brief therapy*. New York: Norton.
de Shazer, S. (1991). *Putting differences to work*. New York: Norton.
de Shazer, S. (1999). *Beginnings*. Retrieved June 18, 1999, from www.brief_therapy.org
de Shazer, S., & Berg, I. K. (1992). Doing therapy: A post-structural re-vision. *Journal of Marital and Family Therapy, 18*(1), 71–81.
de Shazer, S., & Dolan, Y. (2007). *More than miracles: The state of the art of solution focused brief therapy*. New York: Haworth.
de Shazer, S., Berg, I. K., Lipchik, E., Nunnally, E., Molnar, A., Gingerich, W., & Weiner-Davis, M. (1986). Brief therapy: Focused solution development. *Family Process, 25*(2), 207–221.
Dolan, Y., & Nelson, T. (2007). This job is so demanding: Using solution focused questions to assess and relieve burnout. In T. Nelson & F. Thomas (Eds.), *Handbook of solution focused brief therapy: Clinical applications* (pp. 249–266). New York: Haworth.
Dolan, Y. (1991). *Resolving sexual abuse: Solution focused therapy and Ericksonian hypnosis for sexual survivors*. New York: Norton.
Erikson, E. (1950). *Childhood and society* (17th ed.). New York: Norton.
Gergen, K. J. (1985). The social constructionist movement in American psychology. *American Psychologist, 40*, 266–275.
Geyerhofer, S., & Komori, Y. (2004). *Integrating poststructuralist models of brief therapy*. Retrieved April 14, 2008, from www.bssteuropeanreview.org
Gordon, D., & Meyers-Anderson, M. (1981). *Phoenix: Therapeutic patterns of Milton Erickson*. California: Meta.
Haley, J. (1963). *Strategies of psychotherapy*. New York: Norton.
Haley, J. (Ed.) (1967). *Advanced techniques of hypnosis and therapy: Selected papers of Milton H. Erickson*. New York: Grune and Stratton.
Hammond, D. C. (1990). *Handbook of hypnotic suggestions and metaphors*. New York: Norton.
Hospice Association of America. (2003). *Hospice: An HAA/NAHC historical perspective*. Retrieved August 13, 2008, from www.nahc.org
Jones, W. T. (1969). *The classical mind: A history of Western philosophy*. New York: Harcourt, Brace & World.
Kato, P. M., & Mann, T. (1999). A synthesis of psychological interventions for the bereaved. *Clinical Psychology Review, 19*, 275–296.
Kohut, J., & Kohut, S. (1984). *Hospice: Caring for the terminally ill*. Springfield: Charles C. Thomas.
Korman, H. (1997). *On the ethics of constructing realities*. Retrieved May 21, 2008, from www.sikt.nu
Korman, H. (2004). *The Common Project*. Retrieved May 21, 2008, from www.sikt.nu
Kübler-Ross, E. (1969). *On death and dying: What the dying have to teach doctors, nurses, clergy and their own families*. New York: Macmillan.
Kübler-Ross, E. (1975). *Death: The final stage of growth*. London: Prentice-Hall.
Kübler-Ross, E., & Kessler, D. (2005). *On grief and grieving: Finding the meaning of grief through the five stages of loss*. New York: Scribner.
Lambert, M., Shapiro, D., & Bergin, A. (1986). The effectiveness of psychotherapy. In S. Garfield & A. Bergin (Eds.), *Handbook of psychotherapy and behavior change* (3rd ed., pp. 257–310). New York: Wiley.

Lambert, M. J. (1992). Implications of outcome research for psychotherapy integration. In J. C. Norcross & M. R. Goldried (Eds.), *Handbook of psychotherapy integration.* New York: Basic.

Larson, D., & Hoyt, W. (2007). What has become of grief counseling? An evaluation of the empirical foundations of the new pessimism. *Professional Psychology: Research and Practice, 38*(4), 347–355.

Marias, J. (1967). *History of philosophy.* New York: Dover.

McNulty, E. G., & Holderby, R. A. (1983). *Hospice: A caring challenge.* Springfield: Charles C. Thomas.

Miller, G., & de Shazer, S. (1998). Have you heard the latest rumor about...? Solution focused therapy as a rumor. *Family Process, 37*(3), 363–377.

Miller, G., & de Shazer, S. (2000). Emotions in solution focused therapy: A re-examination. *Family Process, 39*(1), 5–23.

Miller, S., Duncan, B., & Hubble, M. (1997). *Escape from Babel: Toward a unifying language for psychotherapy practice.* New York: Norton.

Neimeyer, R. A. (2000). Searching for the meaning of meaning: Grief therapy and the process of reconstruction. *Death Studies, 24,* 541–558.

O'Hanlon, W. H. (1987). *Taproots: Underlying principles of Milton Erickson's therapy and hypnosis.* New York: Norton.

Pattison, E. M. (1977). *The experience of dying.* Englewood Cliffs, NJ: Prentice-Hall.

Romanoff, B., & Thomspon, B. (2006). Meaning construction in palliative care: The use of narrative, ritual, and the expressive arts. *American Journal of Hospice and Palliative Medicine, 23*(4), 309–316.

Rosen, S. (1982). *My voice will go with you: The teaching tales of Milton H. Erickson.* New York: Norton.

Siebold, C. (1992). *The hospice movement: Easing death's pains.* New York: Twayne.

Simon, J. (2005). Three case studies. In T. Nelson (Ed.), *Education and training in solution focused brief therapy* (pp. 149–154). New York: Haworth.

Simon, J., & Berg, I. K. (2004). Solution focus brief therapy with adolescents. In F. Kalsow (Series Ed.) & R. F. Massey (Vol. Ed.), *Comprehensive handbook of psychotherapy: Vol. 3. Interpersonal/humanistic/experiential* (pp. 133–152). New York: Wiley.

Simon, J., & Nelson, T. (2002). Results of last session interviews in solution focused brief therapy: Learning from clients. *Journal of Family Psychotherapy, 15*(4), 27–45.

Simon, J., & Nelson, T. (2007). *Solution focused brief practice with long-term clients in mental health services: I am more than my label.* New York: Haworth.

Stolberg, S. G. (1999). *A conversation with Dame Cicely Saunders: Reflecting on a life of treating the dying.* Retrieved May 23, 2008, from www.nytimes.com

Thomas, F., & Nelson, T. (2007). Assumptions and practices within the solution focused brief therapy tradition. In T. Nelson & F. Thomas (Eds.), *Handbook of solution focused brief therapy: Clinical applications* (pp. 3–24). New York: Haworth.

Walter, J., & Peller, J. (1992). *Becoming solution focused in brief therapy.* New York: Brunner/Mazer.

Watzlawick, P., Weakland, J., & Fisch, R. (1974). *Change: Principles of problem formation and problem resolution.* New York: Norton.

Wittgenstein, L. (1922). *Tractatus logico-philosophicus.* Retrieved June 6, 2008, from www.gutenberg.org

Wittgenstein, L. (1958). *Philosophical investigations* (3rd ed.). New York: Macmillan.

Index

Acceptance
   of death, 4, 82, 83, 84, 89, 108–109, 110
   of exceptions, 174
   of the present, 121, 122
Aikenhead, Mary, 5
Anderson, H., 44, 45, 59
Anthropology, vs. psychology, 25–26
Assumptions, solution focused, 59–60, 119

Bateson, G., 25, 26
Bavelas, J.B., 56
Beckett, S., 107
Benton, R., 109
Bereavement counseling, 41, 49, 55, 63, 102–103, 154–156
   with bereaved family, 141
      co-constructing solutions and effects, 146–149
      individual as part of social systems, 150
      scaling, 150–153
   with bereaved client, 157
      co-construction, 162–164
      E.A.R.S., 170–178
      exception, 161–162
      grieving process, 160–161
      preempting problem talk, 167
Berg, I. K., 23, 26, 27, 28, 29, 30, 31, 32, 38, 44, 59, 64, 67, 70, 71, 78, 132, 170, 172
Berger, J., 25, 26

BFTC. *See* Brief Family Therapy Center
Bonjean, M., 28
Breuer, J., 49
Bridging statement, 92, 94
Brief Family Therapy Center (BFTC), 27–29, 72
Brief Therapy Center, 25–26
Brief versus short-term counseling, 68–69
Butcher, J., 69

Cade, B., 24
Campbell, J., 29, 51
Cantwell, P., 48
Case studies
   local community perspective on hospice, 8–13
   state and national perspective on hospice, 13–21
Cathartic method, of psychotherapy, 49, 50
Center for Solution Focused Brief Therapy Training, 31
Centers for Medicare and Medicaid Services (CMS), 7
Certificate of Need (CON), 8, 10
Change, 65, 76, 119–120, 138, 149–150, 156
   co-construction, 73, 94, 172
   of context, 44
   first order, 61
   future, 78

Change—*Continued*
  inevitable, 58, 60–61
  power for, 72
  second order, 61, 62
Church, Frank, 6–7
Clarity, 72, 113
  of goal, 79–80, 89, 154
Clinicians and clients,
    relationship, 44–45, 48, 53,
    54, 64–65, 73
  mutuality, 77
Client's resources, observation and
    utilization of, 24–25
Clinical engagement, 76–77
CMS. *See* Centers for Medicare and
    Medicaid Services
Co-construction, 44, 45, 50, 58, 61,
    89, 94, 108, 125, 163
  change, 73, 94, 172
  and exceptions, 56, 133
  of goals with clients, 70, 139
    benefiting client and clinician,
      37, 72–73
    within client's life context, 71
    concrete and measurable, 72
    hard work, 73
    important to client, 70–71
    positive expression, 71
    power for change, 71–72
  power of, 48
Cogito ergo sum, 43
Cognitive distortions, 53
CON. *See* Certificate of Need
Conceptual model, of therapy, 26
Conflict, 114, 119
  interpsychic, 43, 52, 53
Connecticut Hospice, 6
Cooperation
  of client, 25–26, 66
  of clinician, 58, 123
  in family, 119, 123
Coping questions, 91
Cost effectiveness, of hospice care, 7

Counseling
  bereavement counseling. *See*
      Bereavement counseling
  brief versus short-term counseling,
      68–69
  role of emotions in, 48–50
Customership, counseling
    relationship, 73

Davis, M. W., 28
Deconstruction
  of complexity, 61
  concept of, 60–61
  of notion of change, 65
  of problem, 75, 85, 94, 139,
      174, 175
De Jong, P., 102
Denial of impending death, 108–109
Department of Health (DOH), 15,
    16, 17, 18
Depression, 48, 144
  clinical, 41
Descartes, R., 43
de Shazer, S., 23, 28, 29, 31, 37, 39,
    42–45, 49, 50, 60, 62, 65, 66,
    68–70, 73, 77, 83, 101, 119,
    127, 131
  client's resources, observation and
      utilization of, 24–25
  cooperation of patient, 25–26
Diagnosis, purpose of, 53
Differentiation problem, 42
DOH. *See* Department of Health
Dolan, Y., 68, 175

E.A.R.S. (elicit, amplify, reinforce
    and start again), 170–178
Emotions in counseling, 48–50
  as separate from contexts, 50
Empathy, in therapy, 175
Erickson, M., 24–25, 67, 82, 95
Erikson, E., 125
Euthanasia, 17

Index

Exception questions, 28–29, 65–66, 85–86

Family therapy, 25
Fields, F., 17
Finiteness, of life, 125
Fisch, R., 25
Five stage concept, for normalizing dying experience, 109–111
Focused problem resolution model, 28–29
Focused solution development model, 29
Formulation, definition of, 56
Foster, Z., 21
Freud, Sigmund, 43, 49, 64
Fry, W., 25
Future oriented questions, 78

Gaetz, D., 17
Gallagher, D., 29, 30, 51, 131
Gates, D., 8, 19
Geyerhofer, S., 43
Gingerich, W., 28, 29
Goal, of therapy, 121, 125
  clarity of, 79–80, 89, 154
  of client, 129
  co-construction with clients, 70
  and difference, 159
  and direction, 77
  of hospice intervention, 122
  solution focus, 96–97
Goolishian, H., 44, 45, 59
Government Accounting Office (GAO), 7
Grady, D., 8–13

Haley, J., 24, 25
Healing stories, 107
  of courage, strength and determination, 111–114
  final letters, 122–125
  peace, 114–120
  remembrance, 120–122
Health Care Financing Agency (HCFA), 16
Heraclitus, 60
Holmes, S., 48
Hopwood, L.E., 102
Hospice
  historical antecedents, 3–5
  Medicare-certified, 6, 7, 17
  public response to, 12–13, 17
  resistance to, 6, 14, 17
  in 20th century
    movement in United Kingdom, 5–6
    movement in United States, 6–8
  See also Case studies
Hospice and Palliative Care Association of New York State (HPCANYS), 15, 21
Hospice Buffalo, 15
Hospice of Marin, 6
Hospice of Orange and Sullivan Counties, 8, 11, 65, 97
Hospice of Schenectady, 17
Hospice of Westchester, 14, 16
HPCANYS. *See* Hospice and Palliative Care Association of New York State
Hudson Valley Health Systems Agency (HVHSA), 8–9
HVHSA. *See* Hudson Valley Health Systems Agency

Information gathering and giving, 38–39
Interpsychic conflict, 52, 53
Intervention, 25, 29, 38, 54, 67, 75, 122
  choices, 55
  grief, 99
  need for professional, 63
  purpose, 61
  as therapeutic misunderstanding, 174
Irish Sisters of Charity, 5

JACHO. *See* Joint Commission on Accreditation of Health Care Organizations
Jackson, D., 25
Joint Commission on Accreditation of Health Care Organizations (JACHO), 7

Kessler, D., 110
Kohut, J., 3, 5
Kohut, S., 3, 5
Komori, Y., 43
Korman, H., 31, 53, 174
Koss, M., 69
Kübler-Ross, E., 6, 109, 110

Lambert, M., 76, 99
Lamers, W., 6
Language games, 46–48
  noncomplimentary, 48
Language use, in solution focus, 37
  emotions in counseling, 48–50
  language games, 46–48
  poststructuralism, 40, 43–45
  structuralism, 41–43
  theory, 38–41
Larson, D., 99
Life review, 107–108
Lipchik, E., 28

Magno, J., 18, 19
Mahoney, J., 19
Managed care, impact of, 12
Marias, J., 42
Meaning making, 48
  poststructuralism, 40, 43–45
  structuralism, 41–43
Medicare-certified hospices, 6, 7, 17
Mental Research Institute (MRI), 25–26, 28
Miller, G., 23, 83
Miller, S., 59, 70, 76, 78

Miracle Question, 38, 78–85, 96, 112, 114, 121, 123, 132, 149
Molnar, A., 28
Monahan, D. P., 16, 18
Moss, Frank, 6–7
Motivation, for client, 25, 30, 54, 68, 136
MRI. *See* Mental Research Institute

National Cancer Institute, 6
National Hospice Association, 14
National Hospice Medicare Benefit, 8
National Hospice Organization, 19
Nelson, T., 42, 46, 59, 70, 83, 175
New York State Hospice Association (NYSHA), 13, 14, 15, 16, 21
Nunnally, E., 28
NYSHA. *See* New York State Hospice Association

One-way mirror approach, 27, 64
Our Lady's Hospice, 4–5

Pattern disruption. *See* Problem pattern disruption
Pattison, E. M., 110
Peller, J., 59, 70
Plato, 42, 43
Platonic world of forms, 42–43
Problem exceptions, 65–66
Problem pattern disruption, 26
Problem solving
  client motivation, 25, 30, 54, 68, 134
  problem effect exploration, on individual, 53
  problem exploration, 52
  problem naming, 52–53
  vs. solution building, 51–52, 56, 57, 60
  successful/unsuccessful, actions based on, 55
  treatment plan, devisal, 54
  treatment plan, application, 54

Problems, concept of, 65
Poststructuralism, 40, 43–45
Pre-session questions, 77–78
Psychoanalysis theory, 53
Psychotherapy, 24
  cathartic method, 49, 50
  psychodynamic, 25

Reality
  client's version of, 58
  co-constructing, 44, 45
Republic, 42
Resistance of client
  to treatment, 54, 55, 65, 66, 67, 97
Romanoff, B., 108

St. Joseph's Hospice, 5
St. Thomas' Hospice, 5
Saunders, D. C., 5, 6, 18, 19–20
Scaling, 171, 176, 177
  bereavement counseling. *See* Bereavement counseling
  future exceptions, 90
  response, 132–134, 137–138
Scaling questions, 86–91
Selinske, C., 13–21
Sequential progression, dying experience, 109–111
Session break, 26, 91–95
SFBTA. *See* Solution Focused Brief Therapy Association
Shedd, C., 15
Shoemaker, D., 11
Short-term versus brief counseling, 68–69
Siebold, C., 3, 6
Simon, J., 26, 42, 46, 59, 71, 83
Solution-building principles, 55–57
  brief versus short-term counseling, 68–69, 96
  co-constructing goals with clients, 70
    concrete and measurable, 72

  good beginning, need for, 71–72
  hard work to accomplish, 73
  important to client, 70–71
  meaning, for client and clinician, 72–73
  positive vs. negative goals, 71
  realistic goals, 71, 96
customership, counseling relationship, 73
vs. problem solving, 51–52, 56, 57, 60
solution focus. *See* Solution focus
Solution-building tools, 75–76
  client/clinician mutuality, 77
  clinical engagement, 76–77
  coping questions, 91
  direction and goal, questions to set, 77
  exception questions, 85–86
  future oriented questions, 78
  Miracle Question, 38, 78–85, 96, 112, 114, 121, 123, 132, 149
  outcomes evaluation, 97–103
  pre-session questions, 77–78
  scaling questions, 86–91
  session break, 91–95
  trouble shooting, 95–97
Solution focus, 65, 68
  assumptions, 59–67
    advice, 66–67
    change, 60–62
    client's effort, 67
    client's control, 62–63
    client's response, 66
    expert on oneself, 64
    problem exceptions, 65–66
    resources, 63–64
    social systems, 64–65
  with bereaved family. *See* Bereavement counseling
  with bereaved client. *See* Bereavement counseling
  common issues in, 95–97

Solution focus—*Continued*
   counselor becoming client, 97
   customer, 96
   goals, 96–97
   pacing the client, 97
   and dying patient. *See* Healing stories
   historical context, 23
      Brief Family Therapy Center (BFTC), 27–29
      de Shazer, Steve, 24–26
      Insoo Kim Berg, 27
      solution focus and Orange County, New York, 29–32
   language use in. *See* Language use, in solution focus
   solution building. *See* Solution-building principles; Solution-building tools
   as Theory of practice, 40
   with a widowed client, 129
Solution Focused Brief Therapy Association (SFBTA), 31–32
Stoicism, 50
Structuralism, 41–43
Suggestion, 94–95, 135

Tax Equity and Fiscal Responsibility Act (1982), 7
Theories, as focus of therapy, 24–25, 38–41
Therapeutic bonding, 76, 143
Therapeutic conversation, 45
Therapeutic misunderstanding, 174
Therapy relationship, curative element, 76
Thomas, F., 59, 70
Thompson, B., 108
Togetherness, importance of, 117
Toma, D., 5
Treatment plan, revising, 54
Trepper, T., 31

Trouble shooting, in solution focus
   counselor becoming client, 97
   customer, 96
   goals, 96–97
   pacing the client, 97

Unconscious, Freud's concept of, 43
United Kingdom
   hospice movement in, 5–6
United States
   Department of Health, Education, and Welfare task force, 7, 15
   hospice movement in, 6–8. *See also* Case studies
   Senate Special Committee on Aging, 6

Vitas, 8

Wald, F., 6, 18
Walter, J., 28, 59, 70
Watzlawick, P., 25, 65
Weakland, J., 25, 26, 27
Westbrook, H., 19
Westbrook, L., 8
Widowed client, solution focus with a, 129
   change, significance of, 138
   "I don't know" response from client, implications of, 130–132
   motivation problem, 136
   organizing at home, 134–135
   scaling response, 132–134, 137–138
Wittgenstein, L., 26, 37, 39, 40, 44, 45, 49, 108, 160
W.K. Kellogg Foundation, 7
World of Ideas, Plato, 43

Yale University Hospital, 6
Yes-set, 82